William Trant

Six Speeches on Financial Reform

William Trant

Six Speeches on Financial Reform

ISBN/EAN: 9783337297497

Printed in Europe, USA, Canada, Australia, Japan

Cover: Foto ©Suzi / pixelio.de

More available books at **www.hansebooks.com**

SIX SPEECHES

ON

FINANCIAL REFORM.

BY

WILLIAM TRANT,

OF THE FINANCIAL REFORM ASSOCIATION.

LONDON:
LONGMANS, GREEN & CO.
LIVERPOOL: WILLIAM GILLING, 49, LORD STREET.
MANCHESTER: JOHN HEYWOOD, DEANSGATE.

1874.

"As we have therefore opportunity, let us do good unto all men."

S. PAUL (Galatians vi. 10).

CONTENTS.

	PAGE
I.—EVILS OF INDIRECT TAXATION	1
II.—ADVANTAGES OF DIRECT TAXATION	41
III.—THE INCIDENCE OF TAXATION	57
IV.—FREE TRADE	74
V.—THE NATIONAL EXPENDITURE	112
VI.—A PLAN OF DIRECT TAXATION	181
APPENDIX A	202
Do. B	203
INDEX	211

INTRODUCTORY.

THE question of Taxation has been ably and amply dealt with in elaborate treatises on political economy, and in numberless pamphlets of a technical character. The Author is not aware of any work in which the subject is discussed in an elementary manner, and he has therefore less hesitation than he otherwise would have in publishing, for popular reading, that which was spoken to popular gatherings. Whenever figures or statistics are quoted, they are the latest that could be obtained up to the time of going to press, and the speeches have been slightly remodelled so as to give them somewhat of a consecutive character. With these two exceptions, they are precisely as they were delivered in the largest towns in England, when they were spoken in support of the adoption of the following Petition to the House of Commons:—

To the Honourable the Commons of the United Kingdom of Great Britain and Ireland, in Parliament assembled.

The Petition of Inhabitants, adopted at a Public Meeting, and signed by the Chairman, on their behalf,

HUMBLY SHEWETH,—

That in the opinion of your Petitioners an expenditure of upwards of seventy millions annually is greatly in excess of the real requirements of the State, and might be most materially reduced without impairing the efficiency of any branch of the public service.

That the great bulk of the revenue to meet this extravagant expenditure is most improvidently raised, by means of duties of Customs and Excise on the necessaries and comforts of life, the effects of which are to extract from the people very much more than the State receives, to check consumption, restrict home and foreign trade, diminish employment, and impoverish the people.

That the fiscal and commercial reforms inaugurated by the late Sir Robert Peel, and since extended, have proved so eminently beneficial, as to warrant further progress in that direction, not stopping short ultimately of the entire substitution of direct for indirect taxation, and the establishment of perfect freedom of trade.

That, pending the inquiry which must precede such a complete revision of our fiscal system, the duties on Tea, Sugar, Coffee, and other articles of food, ought to be forthwith abolished.

Your Petitioners therefore humbly pray that your Honourable House will be pleased to insist on a substantial reduction of the public expenditure, the institution of an inquiry as to the best mode of providing directly for imperial, as well as for local purposes, and the immediate concession of a free breakfast table for the people.

And your Petitioners, as in duty bound, will ever pray.

ROCK FERRY, CHESHIRE,
    1st *June*, 1874.

I.

Evils of Indirect Taxation.

The petition to the House of Commons which I ask this meeting to adopt, refers to so many important reforms that it would be unwise to attempt the discussion of all of them within the limits of a single speech. I shall make no apology therefore for confining my remarks solely to that section in the body of the petition which complains that the great bulk of the Imperial revenue is most improvidently raised by means of duties of Customs and Excise on the necessaries and comforts of life, the effects of which are to extract from the people very much more than the State receives, to check consumption, restrict home and foreign trade, diminish employment, and impoverish the people. What I have to show therefore is, that so far as the revenue is raised by what is called "Indirect Taxation," it is raised improvidently; that the system of taxing commodities not only increases the burdens of the people, but at the same time diminishes the ability of the people to bear them; and that it taxes the poor in the direct ratio that it pauperises them.

The origin of customs duties is involved in obscurity, though there is ample evidence that they have never been a very favourite mode of raising the revenue. Arbuthnot quotes Strabo, to show " that Britain bore heavy taxes, especially the customs on the importation of the Gallick trade;" but customs do not seem to have been much thought of as a source of revenue until they were introduced by Edward I., who had seen, in the course of his expedition to Palestine, how easily money could be extracted from the people by such means. They were abolished as unconstitutional in the reign of Edward II., and, with this exception, "a free import trade was the undoubted constitutional policy of England for six hundred years after the Conquest." A tyrannical and illegal attempt, however, to levy an obsolete tax, without the consent of Parliament, resulted in a war, the execution of the king, and the overthrow of a dynasty; and the disorganised state of the country after this period gave rise not only to a system of customs duties, but to the still more obnoxious system of excise, of which Blackstone says, that "from its first origin to the present time its very name has been odious to the people of England;" and which is very accurately defined by Dr. Johnson as "a hateful tax levied upon commodities, and adjudged not by the common judges of property, but by wretches hired by those to whom excise is paid."

Class legislation, which stares out from almost every line of the Statute Book, is displayed in the history of Taxation as plainly as in any other section of history. When a parliament of landholders found they had the power to wring from a king, who was only too glad to be crowned at any price, a law converting themselves from land*holders* into land-*owners*, and of shifting their burdens on to the shoulders of the people, they not only had no hesitation in doing so, but they did it in a dishonest, disgraceful, and unscrupulous manner. They not only released themselves from their feudal obligations, and by a tax upon beer, ale, cider, and strong waters, shifted the burden on to the shoulders of the people, but they further enacted that the beer, etc., brewed in houses should be exempt from the tax; thus relieving the rich, and imposing the burden almost entirely upon the cottage homes of England : a discreditable transaction, which, however, has a consoling point, inasmuch as it was carried by a majority of only two.

From that moment the duties of Customs and Excise

increased in number and extent with a frightful rapidity, until, in the reign of George III., taxes became so numerous that there was nothing further left to tax; and although premiums were offered for fresh subjects for taxation, none could be found. This state of affairs is thus graphically described by Sidney Smith: "We must pay taxes upon every article which enters into the mouth, or covers the back, or is placed under the foot; taxes upon everything which is pleasant to see, hear, feel, smell, and taste; taxes upon warmth, light, and locomotion; taxes upon everything on earth, and the waters under the earth; on everything that comes from abroad, or is grown at home; taxes on raw material; taxes on every value that is added to it by the industry of man; taxes on the sauce which pampers man's appetite, and the drug which restores him to health; on the ermine which decorates the judge, and the rope which hangs the criminal; on the brass nails of the coffin, and on the ribands of the bride; at bed or at board, couchant or levant, we must pay. The beardless youth manages his taxed horse with a taxed bridle on a taxed road; and the dying Englishman, pouring his medicine, which has paid seven per cent., into a spoon which has paid thirty per cent., throws himself back upon his chintz bed, which has paid twenty-two per cent., makes his will, and expires in the arms of an apothecary who has paid a hundred pounds for the privilege of putting him to death. His whole property is then taxed from two to ten per cent. Besides the probate, large fees are demanded for burying him in the chancel; his virtues are handed down to posterity on taxed marble, and he is then gathered to his fathers to be taxed no more."

It will easily be seen that this state of things was oppressive and could not last long. In 1840, mainly through the exertions of Mr. J. D. Hume, a movement to remit protective duties began; but it was not until estates became so impoverished that the owners gave them up to the parish because the rates exceeded the rents; it was not until people were reduced to an existence upon fifteen pence a-week (eight thousand of them in the Manchester district alone); it was not until the mills and warehouses were closed, and the ships lay idle in the harbours; it was not until there was a famine in Ireland; it was not until sufficient revenue to meet the national expenditure could not be found, and the whole nation was on the verge of bankruptcy and ruin, that Messrs. Bright and Cobden drove home to the hearts of the people of England the necessity of relieving at any rate one commodity from an impost which was starving the country. The result was, that in 1844 the Corn Laws were abolished, and the back of Protection was broken. Since then many remissions of Indirect Taxation have been made—sometimes with great reluctance, as lately; at other times, by a *coup de main*, as in 1854, when Mr. Gladstone followed the advice of the Financial Reform Association, and swept out of the tariff the duties on no less than four hundred and thirty-two articles at one stroke. It is important to remember that whenever a duty has been partially remitted, there have followed considerable advantages to the people; and whenever one has been entirely abolished, greater benefits still have accrued to both consumers and producers alike; so that at any rate the experience of the past warrants us in asking for further similar reforms in the future.

Well, then, although we are not so oppressively taxed, in a sly and indirect manner, as we have been in former times, yet the great fact still remains that, out of £77,123,469 drawn out of the pockets of the people in the financial year ending 31st March, 1873, no less than £46,936,782 were raised by Customs and Excise; and when it is remembered that of the first sum just mentioned, £5,212,145 were paid to the Post-office, and £978,066 to the Telegraph Service, and are therefore not taxes at all, it will be found that the proportion of the taxes raised in a manner which hinders trade, and is unjust to the people, is so unduly large as to demand a vigorous agitation for speedy relief. I remember that during last Christmas week I noticed a grocer's shop in a poor neighbourhood,—a shop chiefly supported by poor people. The window was tastefully laid out to tempt people to buy "extras" for their Christmas treats. There was a fine display of teas and coffees, carefully separated by barricades of cocoa and chocolate, the appearance of the whole being relieved by currants, figs, raisins, dried fruits, succades, and other dainties. Every article in that shop window was taxed, and I thought, as I saw the poor old women purchasing their stock for the following week, that it was hardly fair they should be allowed, in ignorance, to hand their money over the counter to the tradesman under the impression that they were buying food, when in reality they were not only paying taxes, but also a very heavy percentage for the surreptitious manner in which those taxes were paid by them. In fact, they were being cheated. Then again, when they got into the train to take their purchases home they were taxed again; and when, on the following day, the husband sat down after dinner to his glass of beer or spirits and his pipe, he was taxed again; and if he played a game of cribbage or of whist, he was taxed again. When I saw this, I could not shut my eyes to the fact, that while indirect taxes hardly pressed on the rich, they pressed hardly on the poor; and before the people of this country are taxed on what they eat and drink, it would be merely an act of justice to teach them what Indirect Taxation really is, and then ask them if they are willing to submit to such an iniquitous system, when there are so many better and juster ways of raising the necessary revenue. What would the poor women referred to think if, after making their purchases at proper and legitimate prices, a Custom House officer had stopped them and said, "You have purchased two pounds of groceries. I want one shilling for duty, and sixpence for collecting it." That would make every home in England have an interest in the way the money is raised, as well as the way in which it is spent. Messrs. Cope Brothers, of Liverpool, used to print on their tobacco wrappers a notice, to the effect that in one ounce of tobacco at threepence the value of the tobacco was only three farthings, the rest being for duty and expenses; and if every grocer, tobacconist, and others who deal in taxed articles did the same, they would be bestowing a real benefit on their customers.

The first great evil, then, of Indirect Taxation is, I consider, that it falls entirely on the consumer, and therefore taxes a man, not according to his means, but according to his needs, not according to the money he has in his pocket, but according to the mouths he has to feed. The fundamental principle in all taxation,—viz., that a man should contribute his share of taxation according to his means,—is therefore violated by a tax on a commodity. Further, it violates another principle of just taxation, which is, that a tax should take as little as possible, and keep as little as possible, out of the pocket of the taxpayer beyond what goes to the State. Now what is the fact in regard to Indirect Taxation? Let us suppose that a commodity is imported into this country of the value of two shillings a pound, and that the duty thereon is sixpence a pound. The importer therefore has to pay half-a-crown a pound for the article; and if his trade is to pay him he must realise a profit on all the capital he has advanced; that is to say, not only on the two shillings he has paid for the commodity, but also on the sixpence he has advanced for the duty. In other words, he seeks a profit on the half-crown he has virtually paid for the goods. He obtains this profit from the merchant to whom he sells, and the sixpence duty becomes perhaps sevenpence. Then, again, the merchant sells to the wholesale dealer, and the wholesale dealer to the shopkeeper, and, very often, the shopkeeper to a tradesman in a still smaller way of business; so that when the commodity reaches the consumer he has to pay not only a series of profits on the commodity, but some eightpence or ninepence in order that the Government may get sixpence. The Bonding system, it is true, has somewhat modified the *modus operandi* of this, but not to any appreciable effect, as I shall show hereafter. Now the case I have taken is not a supposititious one at all. It is what actually happens in the consumption of tea. When the duty was reduced to sixpence, the grocers instantly began selling at a reduction of eightpence, thus showing that the bonding system does not annihilate all the profits on a duty. The amount of tea imported for home consumption in 1872 was 127,661,360 lbs, its value being £8,928,184, and the amount charged for duty being £3,191,980, or a percentage of £35 15s. 0¼d. on its value. Now add the wholesale dealers' profits and retailers' profits, and we find that what came into the country at £8,928,184 is sold to the consumer for £17,332,884, while at the very outside it ought to have been sold for £12,667,302, but for the duty. Let there be no mistake about the nature of this grievance. It is no sentimental one. It is a real hardship. Professor Leone Levi, a great authority, has shown that in 1870, when sugar, tea, spirits, beer, and tobacco were imported to the amount of £70,000,000, before they reached the consumer they were raised to the enormous price of £150,000,000, in order that the Government might get £35,000,000, an extra tax upon the consumer of at least £50,000,000. The state of affairs is only a little better now. Even at the risk of wearying you, I will give you one more instance of the enormous cost of collecting Indirect Taxes. I take it from the *Co-operative News*. When £46,000,000 are paid to the Government by means of Customs and Excise, the consumers are made to pay nearly £60,000,000, because every grocer, every tobacconist, beerhouse-keeper, licensed victualler, every wine and spirit-merchant, maltster, and importer of taxed articles is obliged to be a tax-collector, and is left to pay himself for his work by an extra charge upon the articles in which he deals. Now, if we could abolish this roundabout mode of collection, nearly the whole of this enormous sum of £15,000,000 would be saved to the public, and would enable us to find permanent employment for 150,000 extra men who are now idle. But further, from the producer to the consumer it is said there are profits to be added amounting to nearly 33 per cent. At this rate, if we could do without Customs and Excise, we should be able to turn over the capital, and we should benefit the producing and trading classes by increasing their income by nearly £20,000,000 sterling, which, of course, would have to bear its fair share of taxation, but which it would be well able to bear.

The tax on a commodity not only falls upon the consumer, it does more, it also injures the producer. If taxes on a commodity, which can be produced and sold for 2s., bring the price up to 2s. 8d., or even more, of course more money is required to purchase that commodity than would otherwise be the case. That is equivalent to saying that were it not for the tax more of the commodity would be purchased. The tax is therefore unjust to the producer, because it deprives him of a customer. The people are thus impoverished at both ends, so to speak, and duty-free articles are equally double blessings.

Another evil in connection with Indirect Taxation is, that a man never knows how much he is contributing to the revenue. Indeed I have met whole assemblies of men who did not know they paid any taxes at all. Now, if a man does not know how much or how little he contributes to the national revenue, he feels little or no interest in the way in which it is spent; and nothing is so likely to produce extravagant government as the knowledge of the fact on the part of the governors, that they can easily conjure the money they require from the pockets of the people without letting them know how they are bamboozled. I venture to say that no government could raise £70,000,000 a-year in the same way as is now done if the working-classes knew how much they contributed towards it. It is only when they are under the chloroform of Indirect Taxation that they can be bled freely without feeling it till they awake from their stupor.

Another objection to an indirect tax is, that it is a voluntary tax. A tax should be certain in its incidence. All should pay their share, and be unable to evade it. An indirect tax, however, can be shirked. Indeed it is shirked. The teetotaller escapes a large share, and, however much we admire teetotalism, it is certainly no reason why a man should escape his share of the national burdens. Mr. J. H. Raper, the able and energetic agent of the United Kingdom Alliance, stated, at the Social Science Congress at Plymouth, in 1872, that he knew of hundreds,—to be emphatic, he repeated the word hundreds,—of persons who drank no taxed articles whatever, neither tea, coffee, cocoa, beer, nor spirits; who did not smoke, and, indeed, who escaped taxation altogether, except when they bought sweetmeats for their children. Now this is not right, because if Tom and Dick can shirk their shares of the taxes, Bill and Harry have to pay them. A tax that is a voluntary tax is wrong in principle, and is especially unjust when it taxes the beverages of the poor, and leaves the silks and satins and luxuries of the rich almost free.

Having maintained in general terms the propositions with which I began, I will now take the national balance sheet, as prepared by the Financial Reform Association, and see what can be said for or against the various items which make up the vast sum of money extracted from the pockets of the people. First, I will speak of the £18,631,109 which were raised upon spirits in the last financial year. I speak of these first, not only because their importance, fiscally, demands it, but because they are the stumbling-block to "free-trade." A great many well-meaning but deluded men (I use the word in no offensive sense) are free-traders in heart, but they dare not consent to the release of intoxicants from the present high tariff. They think it would be a leap in the dark. Of course, the more intelligent teetotalers, such as Sir Wilfrid Lawson, Mr. J. H. Raper, and some others, do not hold that opinion. They propose other means to lessen the amount of drunkenness, but still I have met with hundreds in the course of this agitation who, while desirous of obtaining the "free breakfast table," will not venture upon "free traffic in liquors." There can be little doubt that it is the drunkard and those that fear him who at present form the great stumbling-block to Free Trade. This must be my apology for speaking on this portion of my subject at greater length than I should otherwise have done.

First, it should be borne in mind that experience proves that the same laws which regulate the consumption of necessaries and comforts do not apply to the consumption of drink and other luxuries. The sale of the former is limited by price. The sale of the latter is limited by the desire of the consumer, which in a great many cases is of extraordinary strength, and in not a few amounting to a frenzy. To attempt to regulate this desire by artificially raising the price of what is desired, both common sense and experience show to be futile. Self-indulgence cannot be regulated by Act of Parliament. Morals improve legislation, but legislation cannot — or at any rate does not — improve morality. The State always fails if it tries to control the habits and propensities of the people. Thus it is that the history of the liquor-traffic legislation from A.D. 995 to the present day is one long list of failures. No licensing or prohibitory Act of Parliament reaches those it was intended to affect in the way intended. Nor can any Act do so, as it cannot grapple with the *desire.* The progress of the Temperance movement in this country proves this. The movement has made most headway amongst the classes least affected by prices. Education and an improved tone in society, not duties of Customs and Excise, are what will lead men to do that which is lawful and right. Mr. John Bright, addressing the House of Commons in 1844, said, "There are honourable members of this House, older than I am, but I am old enough to remember when among those classes with which we are more familiar than with the working people, drunkenness was ten or twenty times more common than it is at present. . . . . If it was possible to make all classes as temperate as those of whom I have just spoken, we should be among the very soberest nations of the earth." More recently, in September, 1872, the present Lord Coleridge made a similar statement to the working men of Plymouth, and he gave an instance which had come within his own experience of an intoxicated rector and a member of a good county family, who, on leaving the table at a dinner-party, stumbled on the stairs, and sorely complained, with a thick utterance, that any gentleman should be so regardless of his guests as to have his drawing-room on a different floor to his dining-room. This sort of thing, happily, belongs to a bygone age; and it is important to remember that duties of Customs and Excise have had no effect in bringing about so desirable an improvement. It would be foolish to maintain that they can have any effect in restricting the sale of commodities among those to whom price is no object. Drunkenness in this country has decreased most among those whose power to get drunk is greatest, but whose inclination or desire to do so, it appears, is least.

The experience of 1735 tells a similar story. Drunkenness was then so rife that the attention of Parliament was excited, and stringent measures were demanded. A committee of the whole House resolved "that the *low price* of spirituous liquors is the principal inducement to the excessive and pernicious use thereof. That in order to prevent this excessive and pernicious use, a discouragement be given thereto by a duty to be laid on spirits sold by retail. That the selling of such liquors be restrained to persons keeping public brandy shops, victualling houses, coffee shops, innholders, and to such surgeons and apothecaries as shall make use of it by way of medicine only." The result of that resolution was the Act of 9th Geo. IV., which provided that spirits should not be sold in less quantities than two gallons without a licence, for which £50 was to be paid, and that 20s. a gallon should be levied upon gin. What was the result? Did drunkenness decrease? Quite the contrary. The attempt to enforce the Act gave rise to great excitement leading to riot and violence. Rebellion and murder were feared, and the troops were called out. The consumption of spirits in England and Wales rose from 10,500,000 gallons in 1733, before the passing of the Act, to 19,000,000 gallons in 1742; and there were within the bills of mortality more than 20,000 houses and shops in which gin was sold by retail. "Within two years of the passing of the Act," says Tyndal, "though 12,000 persons had been convicted of offences against it, it had become odious and contemptible; and policy as well as humanity forced the Commissioners of Excise to mitigate its penalties." The prisons were filled with persons unable to pay the penalties required by law, and dissatisfaction prevailed throughout the country. In 1743, it was given in evidence before a committee of the House of Commons, that the quantity of spirit made for consumption in England and Wales was in —

1733	...	...	10,500,000	gallons.
1734	...	...	13,500,000	„
1740	...	...	15,250,000	„
1741	...	...	17,000,000	„
1742	...	...	19,000,000	„

These quantities were consumed by a population not exceeding six millions, the average consumption per head of the population in 1742 being no less than three gallons. The Government, however, repealed the obnoxious statute of 1736 in 1743, substituted a duty of only 7s. 6d. a gallon at the still head, and reduced the licence to 20s. Notice the result. In 1842, one century later, with this regulation in force, and with a population increased to sixteen millions, the consumption was only 8,166,985 gallons in the year, or only half a gallon per head, showing a diminished consumption of five-sixths. The consumption of spirits at the present time strengthens the view here taken, and indeed shows that the consumption increases with an augmented rate of duty, for in 1871, with a duty of 10s. 5d. a gallon, to say nothing of Excise licences for distilling, retailing, etc., the consumption was 33,059,527 gallons, or an advance since 1842 to 1·06 gallons per head. After this it can hardly be contended that taxation can be employed as a check on intemperance. Teetotalers, therefore, must look to other means of spreading their principles than by artificially raising the price of intoxicating drinks, which, *en passant* be it observed, is a selfish policy, as a great many of them are inveterate smokers, and are eager enough to see tobacco imported, manufactured, and sold without any restrictions whatever. A far better plan is that recommended by Mr. T. E. Cliffe Leslie, viz., "education, inducements to saving by reforms in our land laws, rendering investments in land possible on the part of the poor and tending to an improvement of their houses; and, again, friendlier association on the part of the wealthier classes with the poorer, in order to elevate their habits and tastes."

There is another consideration, which is too often lost sight of. No one can help regretting the vast amount of money squandered at gin-palaces by the working man. *All* his earnings, however, are not so spent. Tea, coffee, sugar, food and clothing are the articles he first purchases, and as Professor Fawcett says, it is only, as a rule, what he ought to have saved which he spends at the public-house. This points to a simple remedy; cheapen the articles which compete with intoxicants. Let tea and whiskey fight the battle on a fair field with no favour, and tea will conquer. Let coffee be cheap, and it will largely supersede the use of intoxicating drinks, as it has done with the poorer classes on the Continent. This is proved to some extent by the fact that sailors on the steamers trading between Liverpool and New York, who, having the option of an allowance of rum, tea, or a pecuniary equivalent, usually reject the rum. It is highly probable, too, that cheaper spirits will not increase the amount consumed *by each individual*. The capacity of a man's stomach is limited. What was the experience of 1872? Although the increased ability to purchase, on the part of the working man, in that year, about which so much was made by teetotalers, resulted in a greater quantity of spirits being consumed than was ever known before, yet the amount consumed per head fell to 0·888 gallon, while in the year 1873 there was a still further decline to 0·875 per head of the estimated population. Indeed it seems to me that the increased consumption is to be accounted for, not so much by increased drunkenness, that is, certain men drinking more than they used to drink, but by some men, hitherto abstainers from spirituous liquors, availing themselves of the opportunity of their improved condition to indulge in a glass or two of spirits. Probably, though not certainly, with duty-free spirits the total amount consumed would be greater than ever, because doubtless many persons would drink who cannot now afford to do so; but this much is certain, that even if those who drink now drank then, they would have to drink very much more indeed before they drank away the extra benefits which duty-free spirits (along with perfectly free-trade) would give them. It has been shown by Professor Kirk, that when a man buys for sixpence a gill of whiskey of the "ordinary drinking strength at which Scotch whiskey is sold," he only really gets one-third of a pennyworth of whiskey, the rest being for water, duty, and other needless adjuncts. Now double that quantity is more than drunkards regularly take at a sitting, so that supposing a man with his last shilling in his pocket entered a public-house, and then reeled home under the influence of a pint of whiskey of the "ordinary drinking strength," instead of being pennyless as now, he would have ninepence or tenpence in his pocket for his wife to spend in such things as the family could enjoy in sober gratification.

The whole question may be regarded, too, from another point of view. The amount raised by indirect taxes in this country was £46,936,782 at the close of the financial year 1873. Now, in other words, this means neither more nor less than that this vast sum is withdrawn from production. It is a sum of money, in reality, "needlessly *advanced* by traders and producers, which ought to be productively employed and reproduced, yielding profits at each turn of the capital," and the realised profits of which alone ought to be taxed. To show what such a sum is capable of doing, it may be remembered that, when wages were not nearly so high as at present, the wages fund averaged £20 a head of the population. On that basis the diversion of the money *advanced* by the trading community into a productive channel would be equal to founding a town of 2,181,455 inhabitants, or larger than Liverpool, Manchester, Birmingham, Leeds, and Glasgow added together, with all the increased material prosperity which such a town would add to the country, and which would be able to bear its share of taxation without restricting trade, and would in fact reduce local and national burdens, by employing a vast number of persons now considered as an idle and surplus population. Truly the question of pauperism cannot be said to have been fairly grappled with while such an enormous amount of labour cries in the streets, and a deaf ear is turned to its earnest supplications. The evil of this withdrawal of capital goes further, too, for, as Mr. Robert Donnell points out, "We can hardly ask the United States to give up their thirty-five per cent. duty on linen if we are to retain our three hundred per cent on their tobacco." Thus, because we tax a luxury, a trade in a necessity or comfort is prevented between two great nations; and so with other countries and other commodities. Indeed, as Mr. T. E. Cliffe Leslie shows, the amount of money advanced as above mentioned is " withdrawn by a system which closes our coasts and rivers to local enterprise and foreign trade, our factories to improvement, and our laboratories to invention; forbids the free cultivation of our fields, creates monopolies, and maintains exorbitant duties on the produce of foreign nations, who retaliate with duties which, by curtailing the market for our manufactures, augment, in accordance with a well-known law, the cost of production, and therefore their price to consumers at home."

There is yet another consideration on this head. It

is one which ought to have great weight with honest men. "It is said," remarks Professor Leone Levi, "that the Emperor of China proudly rejected every consideration of revenue when urged to admit opium at a duty. There was indeed something sublime in his declaration. 'It is true I cannot prevent the introduction of the flowing poison; gain-seeking and corrupt men will for profit and sensuality defeat my wishes, but nothing will induce me to derive a revenue from the vice and misery of my people.'" Now, in this country, teetotalers share with their less rigid compatriots all the advantages of an organised government. The army and navy protect the property of Sir Wilfrid Lawson, as well as that of Mr. Bass. The same police supervision is exercised over the person and property of the one as of the other; and laws are not made for the good of one which do not equally apply to the other. Yet to a very large extent this is paid for by the duties on intoxicating drinks. Is it a just system which allows hundreds of thousands of persons to enjoy the advantages of government, and yet contribute little or nothing towards the cost of that government? Is it not an immoral position in which to be placed, that of sharing the advantages of a government largely paid for out of the sale of that which is the cause of so much misery and vice? That the drunkard should be the "mainstay" of our constitution is, as Sir Wilfrid Lawson pointed out in his speech on the Budget of 1873, "mean, cruel, short-sighted, and fraught with evil to the State." Indeed teetotalers may rest assured that no Government will attempt to legislate effectually on the liquor question as long as such a large sum as the cost of the army and navy is raised from the consumption of drink. The Chancellor of the Exchequer likes a surplus, and if it be legitimate to obtain it from intoxicating drinks, it is equally legitimate for him and his Government to offer greater facilities for their consumption, in order that the surplus may be as large as possible.

The following conclusions, therefore, seem perfectly logical: First, that duties of Customs and Excise do not restrict the sale of intoxicating drinks; secondly, that the best way to do so is to teach men the folly of drunkenness, and as that is a long process, to at once cheapen the articles which compete with intoxicants, in order that policy may dictate what imprudence neglects; and thirdly, that it is not only unjust and impolitic, but highly immoral, to raise a revenue from the consumption of "flowing poisons."

There can be little doubt, I think, that if you would

have a nation less drunk, you must offer it greater encouragement to be more sober; and above all things do not tax those beverages which are among the principal inducements to sobriety with those who *will* drink something or other. It has been well said that the concession of the "Free Breakfast Table" would do more good to the working classes than closing half the gin shops; and would be a greater benefit to the commercial world than the discovery of a gold field. Of course this reasoning leads to the conclusion that it would be better that the consumption of light wines and beer should displace that of spirits to a very large extent. I should not be sorry to see this, and I urge it as an additional reason why the duties should be removed. It is a great pity that there is no pleasant unintoxicating beverage in England, and the nearer we can approach such a thing the better. Indeed, prior to the treaty of Methuen (1703), French wines were drank in this country to a very great extent; but the foolish policy of that treaty developed a taste for the strongly brandied wines of Spain and Portugal,— a method of cultivating taste which may have had something to do with John Bull's liking for ardent spirits at the present day.

Why, in France, where brandy is cheap, I have not

seen as much drunkenness in six months as I can find in the heavily-taxed dram-shops of London in one night; and I am told that in Jersey and Guernsey, where almost every shop is licensed, where rum may be had at twopence-halfpenny and brandy at threepence the half-pint, and a glass of good ale for one penny, there is not a thirtieth part of the drunkenness to be met with which may be found on any similar area in England. Adam Smith says, that if we consult experience the cheapness of wine seems to be a cause, not of drunkenness, but of sobriety. I think, too, that it is worth considering whether it is proper to tax a commodity which is so often recommended by medical men to those patients who can ill-afford to purchase wine, the price of which is artificially enhanced. Every shilling saved from the consumption of wine, and indeed of all other commodities, would be so much added to the fund applicable for general production and employment of labour. I think I need say no more with regard to the impolicy and folly of taxing wines, beer and spirits.

Much of the same reasoning applies to the malt-tax; and setting aside the fact that it is another tax upon the poor, there are other considerations which render it desirable that it should be abolished. It is now admitted that the malt tax prevents the farmer from cultivating his land to the greatest advantage; that it obstructs him in the use of a valuable article of food for cattle, limiting the quantity of meat and dairy produce; that it tends to foster two great monopolies, malting and brewing, by calling for a larger amount of capital to carry them on; that it encourages the adulteration of beer, and prevents to a great extent the habit of home-brewing by the labouring classes. Mr. Joshua Fielden says that in the manufacturing districts 76 per cent. of the householders brewed at home; 8 per cent. would, but could not afford it; 6 per cent. bought their beer at the publichouse, and 10 per cent. did not drink beer. Further, it imposes upon the consumer an additional 45 per cent. on the cost of collecting; according to other authorities, it costs £10,000,000 to collect £6,000,000, and according to others, even still more.

With regard to the duty on tobacco, similar observations apply. Indeed, I pointed out in a debate on this very subject, at the Social Science Congress at Plymouth, in 1872, that according to the publications of the Anti-Tobacco Association, there were quite as sufficient reasons for the suppression of the tobacco trade as for the prohibition of the liquor traffic. I have lately been reading articles by Professor Newman, and other vegetarians, and I am sure a good case is made out against eating meat; while if a man pin his faith to the *Lancet*, he will find quite enough in that journal to frighten him, and make him clamour for a permissive bill to restrict the consumption of tea. The fact is, the consumption of these articles is not a question in which taxation ought at all to interfere. It is a question of a man's own taste.

Of the duty on tobacco I will only say that the "fragrant weed" was grown in Ireland in the reign of William IV., and is said to have yielded £60 to £70 an acre. It was then suppressed by tariffs, which still prevent its cultivation there. It is the natural rotative crop for potatoes, and it is said to prevent the potato disease. It grew in Yorkshire before its cultivation was suppressed, and there can be no doubt that in England and Ireland its cultivation and manufacture would employ thousands of hands. So that here is another industry destroyed.

One remark more before I proceed. If the principle I am advocating be sound, there must be no exceptions. The grounds generally urged for taxing drinks and licensing houses, would apply as well to prostitutes in the one case, and brothels in the other. Are the teetotalers prepared to maintain this doctrine?

If everything which causes evil and wickedness is to be taxed, why not begin with racing and racehorses, and finish off by heavily mulcting the captains of the Oxford and Cambridge crews?

Nor is it wise to tax luxuries. If rich men require carriages, employment is given to body-makers, carriage-builders, wheelwrights, spring-makers, smiths, trimmers, painters, harness-makers, etc., etc., to say nothing of the builders of coach-houses, stables, etc., etc.; and a tax upon carriages restricts all these trades. There is no tax upon carriages in Ireland, and it is a remarkable fact that in that country there are comparatively more handsome vehicles than in this. The same argument applies to the tax upon armorial bearings, which, if abolished, would give greater employment to lapidaries, printers, and others, as indeed the recent reduction of the tax has already done.

I do not propose to mention to you now the advantages of admitting tea free, because I shall have something to say on that subject when I come to treat of the exchange of commodities by various countries. I will simply say that it is cruel on the part of Government to put its hands into the teapot. Tea is drunk, Mr. Dudley Baxter informs us, by the poor at nearly every meal, and it really would be more charitable, if commodities are to be taxed at all, to tax some article of less general consumption. It is really a tax upon poor washerwomen and seamstresses, who ought to have nearly three pounds of tea for the money which now buys one. I do, however, wish to say a word or two in regard to taxing sugar. This is not only used very largely as an article of food, the Irish putting it into everything they eat when they can get it; but were it untaxed a new industry would spring up in England. It has been proved that the climate and soil of Suffolk, and other English counties, are eminently fitted for the cultivation of beet-root, which has been so successful on the continent. The cultivation of this root would not only enable us to produce in this country a great amount of sugar,— say one pound of saccharine matter out of twelve and a half pounds of beet,— but it necessitates and pays for high and enriching farming; and as the pulp is used for cattle food after it is deprived of the water and saccharine matter it contains, it is uniformly attended by a great increase in the production of fat cattle, as well as in the yield of corn. I give this on the authority of Mr. James Caird, who, in spite of the Customs and Excise restrictions, is successfully cultivating this root at Lavenham, in Suffolk. The same gentleman says, "If sugar should come to be regarded as a prime necessary of food, which, like bread, should be untaxed, we might see a very rapid development of sugar culture in England, with advantages to consumer and producer even greater than have everywhere followed its introduction on the continent."

Then, again, Mr. Arnold Baruchson has calculated that if the 300,000 acres of mangold now grown in this country,—to say nothing of acres upon which nothing at all is grown,—were used for the cultivation of beet, the yield might be twenty tons per acre, which would give 6½ per cent. of sugar on the quantity of beet root planted, being an annual value of £17,700,000; whilst the refuse would be applicable to all the purposes of the mangold. I mention these facts because all this is prevented by the duties at present imposed on a commodity which is universally consumed, from the child sucking its lollipop to the countess nibbling her confectionery.

I might go further on this point and show you, as Mr. John Noble has done, that the duty on sugar has a tendency to prevent chemical investigation, as was proved in Dr. Watson Bradshaw's application for a patent for his Dietetic Grape Sugar, a most invaluable medicine. Difficulties were raised by the Excise, and ultimately £12 per ton (the highest in the scale) had to be paid. Just in the same way (for it is the old story over again) a great many new inventions in the manufacture of candles and starch were patented as soon as the duties on those articles were removed.*

It is the same with regard to the cultivation of chicory. Her Majesty's Commissioners of Revenue say, that unless we allow chicory to be grown in this country on better terms than we do at present, we can never compete with the Belgian growers. The cultivation has entirely ceased in Northampton, and the only growing is now confined to the neighbourhood of York. So here is another industry prevented from developing, and employing a large number of men.

With regard to coffee, the same remarks apply as when tea was referred to, though they will have greater force when the people of this country learn how to make a cup of coffee, which would be certain largely to increase the consumption of this delightful and refreshing beverage.

I have now shown you the principal sources from which the revenue is derived. It is not my intention to go into the details or to speak of the minor channels whence the State receives its income. I wish, however, to point out that all our licenses, and some of our

* See Appendix A.

stamps, are indirect taxes, and not direct ones, as is often supposed. The receipt stamp, stamps on bills of exchange, promissory notes, etc., are of this kind. They are not oppressive, but they are very absurd, and have only the merit of convenience. Licenses are different. By the common law of England, any man may carry on any lawful business whatever. Statute law, however, steps in and stigmatises some trades as licensed trades, and in this it is very capricious. For instance, Why should a man require a license to sell silver spoons, but not to sell silver watches? What great crime has an auctioneeer, or an appraiser, or a pawnbroker, or a banker, or an attorney committed that he should require permission to trade, and should have to pay for that permission? Why should a man who makes playing cards be taxed, when the man who makes billiard tables, balls and cues is not? And what more harm is there in making vinegar than in selling lemons, and yet one is taxed and the other not. The tax on railway passengers and railway carriers is a tax on locomotion; the license to carry guns restricts the Birmingham trade, and so contemptible is this tax in the eyes of those who have guns, that the Commissioners of Inland Revenue have been obliged to issue notices that hereafter the names of those who have paid their license will be affixed twice a year on the church doors of their parish, as a warning and intimation to those who have not paid. I am not now contending that the State should interfere with no trades—that there should be no licenses. It may be necessary that there should be "rules of the road" on sea and land to prevent collisions; it may be necessary to license certain men as lawyers and doctors to prevent quackery and deception; it may be necessary to license even omnibus and cab drivers; and it would probably be better if qualified men were licensed as railway directors. What I am contending for is, that no revenue should be so raised. It is not fair to tax a man's trade. It is an indirect tax upon his customers. It harasses trade and gives rise to endless annoyance. If I wanted proof of the way in which trade is harassed I should ask any sugar importer, and he would tell me—as I have often been told—that always as the time of the introduction of the Budget approaches, it is dangerous to buy, and therefore no one can sell. It is expected the trade will be meddled with in some way or other, and so in the sugar market there is an annual panic. Look, too, at the various associations continually waiting upon members of the government. There are the Tea Dealers and Grocers, the Beer and

Wine Trade Societies, the Licensed Victuallers, and a host of others, all crying out that their trades are harassed, but you never hear of any association being organised to ask the government to impose duties on cottons, or upon any other commodities. The unfettered trades are content.

Then there is the immorality which the system gives rise to. Men smuggle; they see no crime in it, nor do I. As Dryden said,—

> " Customs to steal is such a trivial thing
> That 'tis their charter to defraud their king."

A great quantity of tobacco is smuggled into this country, more than you think of. I know whole families who smoke nothing else but smuggled tobacco. It comes into Liverpool daily. It comes concealed in bales of hops, in casks of potatoes, even inside loaves of bread. Men are fined and imprisoned, and yet it goes on day after day and week after week. There are not so many illicit stills in England now, but this is accounted for by the general prosperity of the country rather than anything else. Probably they number a few scores; in Ireland they may be counted by hundreds, and the men, when detected, can afford to pay the penalty instead of going to prison, and having so paid they begin operations again. "And surely," in the language of Sir Robert Walpole, "it must be considered an intolerable grievance, that by the frauds which are daily committed, the very poorest of the peasantry are obliged to pay this duty twice, once in the enhanced price of the articles,—for, though the fraudulent trader contrives to save to himself the amount of the tax imposed by Parliament, yet he does not sell it cheaper to the public,—and a second time in the tax that is necessarily substituted to make good the deficiency which has by these means been occasioned." To which we may add, that the fair trader's profit is diminished by exposure to unequal competition with the smuggler.

There is another thing. In the case of sugar you know the duties are levied according to the quality. If a ship have a cargo of the best quality, it will save the owner several hundreds of pounds to have it passed as an inferior quality. It is worth his while, therefore, to slip a fifty pound note into the hands of the Custom House officer, and so get his goods passed. I need hardly say this is often done, and this is how it is that Custom House officials, with £150 and £200 a-year, are enabled to reside in very big houses, and live at a very fast rate. It is as true in principle

to-day as when Swift wrote: "Some Custom House officers, birds of passage, and oppressive thrifty squires, are the only thriving people among us." One instance of the immoral effects of taxing commodities may be seen to-day at any American port. In consequence of the high tariffs existing in that country, nearly every subordinate officer, on nearly every ship trading between Liverpool and New York, takes out with him portable goods, so as to cheat the Custom House, by trading on his own account. To such an extent is this carried on that Liverpool firms keep agents specially for looking after this branch of their business. Only the other day I cut this advertisement out of a Liverpool newspaper:—
"Wanted, an experienced young man to solicit orders amongst Officers, Stewards, and others for a first-class and wholesale Tailoring Establishment. Must have good references and be well acquainted with the business.—Address," etc. Coats, shirts, etc., which the customer can take out on his back, are sent over in large quantities; while umbrellas are especial favourites on account of their portability. Indeed, it is a standing joke in America that in consequence of the high duties paid on umbrellas they are national property, and may be walked off with from the passage-stands with impunity, as no magistrate will commit. Duties of Customs

and Excise, then, give rise to deception, lying, and worse crimes, and engender a contempt for law, which is the next thing to creating a contempt for those who make the laws and those who administer them.

I have now redeemed my promise. I have shown you that Indirect Taxation is unjust to the producer, because it robs him of customers; it impoverishes the people, because it restricts their means of living; it cheats them, because it taxes them without their knowing it; and it takes from the labourer more than the State requires, and for which, therefore, the State gives him no return, thus reducing his wages by that amount. It restricts commerce, harasses trade, and creates monopolies. Finally, the great vice of Indirect Taxation is not only that it is unjust and unequal, but that it limits, restricts, and hampers beneficial exchange; it harasses and prevents a thousand operations of industries, which, when called into existence, would assist to spread abundance, contentment, and morality amongst the people of this country; and if England abolished such a clumsy and iniquitous system she would set an example of wisdom and justice to all the nations of the earth.

II.

ADVANTAGES OF DIRECT TAXATION.

Lord Macaulay wrote: "The discontent excited by direct taxes is, indeed, always out of proportion to the quantity of money which they bring into the exchequer." This, it seems to me, is the great recommendation of a direct tax. It gives rise to an "impatience of taxation," as it has been aptly called. With a system of direct taxation, every man would have a notion he was paying too much, and he would enquire into the circumstances of the case. He would want to know how the money was spent, and why he had to pay more than another man. Let the nation once do this, and the days of unjust taxation would be cut short, and a system with a just incidence established. It is a foolish thing for a nation to pay taxes and not know that it does so, for then the governors will keep it equally in the dark as to how they spend them. I have therefore no hesitation in asking you to adopt a petition to Parliament, praying for an alteration in the mode of raising the revenue, from an indirect method to one entirely and completely direct.

I will premise, however, that people often fall into the fallacy of believing that because direct taxation is a good thing, and all indirect taxes bad, therefore that all direct taxes are good. This is an error. A poll tax is a direct tax, but it is not a good one. It is neither equal nor just. So also Schedule D of the Income Tax is a direct tax; but it is inquisitorial, oppressive, and demoralising. All direct taxes are not good, and are not just; but of this you may be quite sure, that no tax that is good or that is just is any other than a direct one. All direct taxation is not just taxation, but all just taxation is direct.

It is a remarkable fact that the ruling classes, when they made war in bygone days did so not for the people but for themselves. Few wars have ever been made for the people. Formerly the class which legislated was the class which fought, and what was more, it was the class which paid. They therefore made war in the full consciousness that they would have to pay for it. The result was, that a national debt was a thing unheard of. It was not until we had indirect taxation that our rulers were able to run us into debt. I am quite convinced that if during the last century we had had direct taxation, the people of this country would not have entered upon wars which were of no earthly or heavenly use. John Bull would think thrice before he doubled the Income Tax, or any other tax that he had to pay in hard coin, while he would know little of it if it were concealed in his beer and tea. With direct taxation there would be no such thing as a war-fever. Why, in 1860, the then Lord Derby opposed direct taxation on the very ground that, to use his own words, it would be so "odious that war will be avoided, because no party will incur the odium of carrying it on." "They say," he said, "they will secure peace, by taking away the power of making war." As it is, the people of this country — especially the poor people — have to pay for wars not one of which they approve now, or would have approved when they were waged, if they had known the expense they were entailing upon themselves. It seems to have been the notion of England that it ought to mix itself in every quarrel on the face of the earth; that its arms were invincible — which they were not; that it must win all the battles — which it did not; that it would get all the glory — which it could not; and then that it would pay all the expenses — which it succeeded in a great measure in doing. Mr.

Andrew Bissett pointed out this some time ago. From the time of the Norman dynasty to the restoration of Charles II., a period of 594 years, the period of Direct Taxation, "England kept her national defences in so complete a state that no foreign power dared to attempt invading her; and carried on, besides, a vast number of great wars, in the course of which she planted her flag on the walls of Acre, made one King of France prisoner and dethroned another, restored a King of Spain to his throne, destroyed the Spanish Armada, and finally made the name of Englishmen as much respected over the world as that of the Romans had been. And all this she did without contracting a farthing of debt." Then, however, came indirect taxation, and the burdens were shifted on to the shoulders of the people. "From the restoration of Charles II. to the year 1815 is a period of 155 years. During that comparatively short time (little more than a fourth of the former), England, — in carrying on wars which should certainly not have cost her greater efforts than those above referred to; in making war for the Dutch; for the succession of the crown of Spain; in making war first for, and then against, the House of Austria; in conquering Canada; in losing America; in the wars of the French Revolution; and, in the course of all this, subsidising more than half Europe,—contracted a debt of upwards of eight hundred millions, while taxes to an enormous amount were levied on the labouring and commercial class of the community." To all this is to be added the Crimean war, where we got a treaty which is now repudiated; the Alabama difficulty, which was brought upon us by the iniquitous conduct of British shipbuilders; and the Abyssinian war, into which officialism drifted us; to say nothing of the China war, which might have been avoided; the various Indian mutinies, for which in a great measure we were to blame; and the Ashantee war, about which we know nothing yet; and I think you will agree with me that Conservatives, at any rate, ought to be in favour of direct taxation, as it is neither more nor less than "recurring to their original policy."

It was for carrying on such a policy as this, then, that the people of this country have now to pay the expenses. Mr. C. E. Macqueen, the indefatigable Secretary of the Financial Reform Association, whose energy, earnestness, and zeal, are only equalled by the indomitable perseverance and immunity from fatigue with which a sincere, hearty faith in his cause alone can inspire a man, is always making extraordinary calculations, by way of removing the difficulties of the mind in conceiving the meaning of stupendous figures, and converting the monotony of page after page of statistical tables from mere shower-baths of figures into telling facts. Amongst other things he has pointed out that if thirty millions of people, which is nearly the population of the United Kingdom, were passing the edge of an abyss in single file, at the rate of one per minute, and if each of them "threw in £279 odd, it would take upwards of fifty-seven years, day and night, without intermission, before the sum spent on war and war debt from 1688 to 1872 could be got rid of in a way about as beneficial as that in which it has been expended." Let every taxpayer remember this. Let every taxpayer remember that of every pound he pays in taxes, whether directly as income tax, or indirectly by tobacco and coffee, no less than 14s. 9¾d. is expended for war and war debt, and only the remaining 5s. 2¼d. for the cost of Civil Government. With this borne in mind — and direct taxes would drive it home — and with the future revenue of this country raised by direct imposts, I am quite sure that however much the passions of the people might be roused, however anxious the rulers of the land might be to involve us in national disputes, whether under the name of a vigorous foreign policy, or by any other title, the people of this country would think twice when they remembered how deeply they would have to thrust their hands into their pockets. Men would then see that it was to their interest to remain at peace, and when the majority of a nation once feels that, there will be no war.

Direct taxation, however, is not only a check upon war expenditure, but it is a preventive of all other extravagance. "If," says Mill, "all taxes were direct, taxation would be much more perceived than at present; and there would be a security which now there is not for economy in the public expenditure." I have pointed out that when the legislators were also the taxpayers, and knew it, we had economical government. At present, our legislators — the Lords and Commons — pay much less than their fair share of the national burdens, and they are well aware of the fact. They have not, therefore, the inducements to be economical which they ought to have, as an extravagant expenditure falls more lightly upon them than upon the people. With direct taxation, however, they would be obliged to pay their due share, and personal motives, if nothing else, would make them look after their own interests, and in doing that they would be respecting the interests of the nation. "In the days of our laborious ancestors," once said the *Morning Star*, "taxation was direct, and was taken from the rich. Since we have become civilised we have made taxation indirect, and the poor pay a proportion of taxes one-fourth of which would have caused a rebellion among their richer ancestors." The Americans have found this out. Recently, in a memorial to Congress from the Taxpayers' Convention of South Carolina, complaining of the "schemes of public plunder which have been openly advanced by corrupt measures," it was pointed out that a majority of the members of the Legislature owned no portion whatsoever of the property taxed, and the remaining portion owned so little that their pay as members constituted their entire interest as property-holders. The result is, that those owning the property having no voice in the Government, and those imposing the taxes having no share in the burden thereof, the taxes have advanced yearly, until, in many cases, they consume more than one-half of the income from the property taxed.

We should be more economical if we realised the fact that when John Bull is thrusting his hands into his pockets, he is really spending our money. "If," says Hosea Biglow, " by means of direct taxation, the bills for every extraordinary outlay were brought under our own immediate eye, so that, like thrifty housekeepers, we could see where and how fast the money was going, we should be less likely to commit extravagances. At present, the poor man is charged as much as the rich; and whilst we are saving and scrimping at the spigot, the Government is drawing off at the bung. If we could know that a great part of the money we pay in tea, sugar, coffee, and tobacco, goes to buy powder and ball, and in keeping a lot of idle sinecurists, it would set some of us a-thinking." An overflowing revenue is always an inducement to spend. It corrupts both the governors and the governed. The former invent channels of extravagant patronage, the latter expect golden prizes. "A revenue rigorously proportioned to the wants of the people is as much as can safely be trusted to men in power."

I say, then, that a direct tax is a good tax, because it is a provocative to economy. Another great advantage is, that it will always have a tendency to fall upon the right shoulders. Nothing has pleased me more than the discontent to which the income tax has given rise. There have been cries on all sides that it is unfairly levied, that men are made to pay on larger incomes than they really have; and, indeed, so obnoxious is the whole affair, that a powerful organisation has been formed to agitate for its removal. Why, gentlemen, if the same amount of taxation had been wrung from these complaining tradesmen by taxes on the commodities they consumed, they would never have known they were overtaxed. Why should we require the pill of taxation to be gilded? It is the fact that hard cash has been demanded from them, that they have had to open their purses and actually pay the taxgatherer in money, which has made them feel the unjust incidence of the tax; and if the whole of the revenue was raised thus directly, and of course more justly assessed, the nation itself would see that the tax was properly apportioned.

Then, again, a direct tax is cheaper to collect. To pay a direct tax costs nothing more than the tax itself, and the cost of collecting it; and this latter item is or should be a very small per centage.

Under an equitable system, there would be no inducements to adulterate, and therefore the expense of a detective force would be avoided; there would be no more smuggling, and therefore the cost of the Revenue cruisers all around the coasts would be saved. It would do away with the enormous expense of the Custom House system; it would abolish the Exciseman, and reduce the staff of Revenue officers, and thus not only cause a sensible reduction in the price of every article that is consumed, but would enable the taxes to be collected at a cost of about 1½ or 2 per cent., instead of about a cost of 25 per cent. as at present. If anyone wishes to be convinced of the absurd, clumsy, anomalous way of collecting the taxes by means of Custom Houses, let him study the return which Mr. James White, the member for Brighton, succeeded in persuading the Government to issue in 1872. It is a return of the total costs of the Customs for the year 1870. Only one similar return has been granted before, and that was in 1870, and referred to 1868, and it is astonishing how much alike these returns are. Of course, you are aware that all places on the coasts of our island are not ports, that is to say, they cannot carry on a foreign trade, however much they may wish to do so. Her Majesty's Commissioners of Customs have selected 133 places to which the privilege is granted. I do not know what has guided these gentlemen in the selection they have made. Doubtless, in the plenitude of their wisdom, they have had sufficient grounds for all they did; but the state of affairs is anything but satisfactory. In 36 out of these 133 ports, the cost of collecting is double the amount collected; twenty-eight of them collect

£9,196, and the cost of doing it is £26,123, or a cost of £3 for every £1 collected. In fact, there are only about nineteen of them at all worth keeping up, and in these the cost is never less than £1 10s. per cent., and it ranges from that figure to 100 per cent. Who would have thought, for instance, that at a port like North Shields, it costs £30 8s. 5¾d. per cent. to collect the Customs' duties; at Cardiff, £55 8s. 2½d. per cent.; and those who have seen the busy appearance of the port of Hartlepool, the activity of the Custom House officers, and the great shipping trade that seems to be done there, will doubtless be surprised to hear that the amount collected there in 1870 was £5,583, and that the cost of collecting it was £5,631 6s. 3d., or £100 7s. 2¼d. per cent.; that is to say, that at Hartlepool the Custom House did not collect a sufficient amount of duty to pay its own expenses. The case of Fleetwood is still worse; while at Milford Haven, which I remember my school Geography described as "the finest natural harbour in the world," the cost of collection was £1,340 17s. 4d., and that was spent to collect the enormous sum of £4, which was at the rate of £33,521 13s. 4d. per cent. There are even worse cases, and the whole temple of anomalies is finally crowned with the amusing but disgraceful fact, that at

Aberystwith, Cardigan, Guernsey, Jersey, Kirkwall, Maldon, Padstow, Stranraer, and Wigton, the total cost of the Custom Houses was £6,778 4s. 4d., and there was not a single penny collected, all the work done being the restriction of trade as much as possible. The total cost of the collection of the Customs dues was £787,876 11s. 1d., which was nearly four per cent. on the amount collected. Well, this peculiar state of things must exist as long as the taxes are collected with such a clumsy contrivance as the Custom House. With a system of direct taxation, this would be done away with, and in addition to the saving thus effected, trade would be allowed to expand as much as possible. For, while indirect taxation cramps and prevents trade, any steps towards direct taxation relieve it, and allow it to expand. From 1842 to 1866, there were repealed or reduced Customs or Excise duties to the net amount of £19,692,895; and during the same period the revenue derived from these two departments increased from £35,667,679 in 1842, to £42,973,000 in 1866. The amount of prosperity here shown is very great, and I am quite sure that with further reforms in the same direction equally great benefits will follow. As Voltaire says, "Taxes are necessary; the best mode of levying them is that which most facilitates labour and commerce."

Again, a tax is a payment for services rendered by the State, from which every individual ought to derive an equal benefit. The tax ought, therefore, not only to be equitably assessed, but deemed as obligatory as any other payment for services rendered. Now, all indirect taxes can be entirely or in part avoided and shifted on to one's neighbours, without the neighbours knowing it, while a direct tax, equitably assessed, must fall upon the parties intended. "The certainty of what each individual ought to pay," says Mill, "is in taxation a matter of so great importance, that a very considerable degree of inequality, it appears, I believe from the experience of all nations, is not near so great an evil as a very small degree of uncertainty." Adam Smith expresses a similar opinion; and again, Dr. Chalmers: "A free people ought to know what they pay for freedom, and should scorn to be cheated into paying for it."

I am aware that the immediate substitution of direct taxes would be unpopular. People have been so used to paying without knowing it, that it would be some time before they became reconciled to the visits of the tax-gatherer *in propria persona*. But I am equally sure that when once a man realises the real advantages of a just system he must infinitely prefer it to being fleeced in the price of commodities; and as

Handel Cossham says, "If a man knows what he pays, he is anxious to know *why* he pays." With direct taxation, from half a dozen to a score of members of Parliament, always with a majority of officials, would no longer be left at one, two, or three o'clock in the morning, as at present, to vote away millions of the public money in an extravagant and merciless manner.

I say, then, in conclusion, that direct taxation is the only proper and equitable mode of raising a revenue. To say that it is impracticable is absurd in the face of the fact that our local rates are nearly all raised in that manner, and no sane man would wish that the municipal rates should be raised by taxes on commodities. A direct tax is in accordance with the canons of taxation. It takes no more out of the tax-payers' pockets than is required by the State, with a minimum cost of collection added; it is the only kind of tax that can be equitably adjusted; under it a man knows what he pays, and can therefore discover if he pay too much; it is the only check upon the extravagance of the Government: and it releases trade from the shackles which enslave it.

"Instead of taxing Nature, let us tax ourselves." Let us have no more taxes on trade; they are the barbarous contrivance of a barbarous age, when the industrious were outside the pale of the constitution, and only warriors were within it. They are the deadly enemies of production, of manufacture, and the free intercourse of nations; they are opposed to the interests of peace, and to the progress of civilisation, and they are unworthy the days of the Electric Telegraph, the Suez Canal, the Mont Cenis Tunnel, and the Great Pacific Railway. Let us remove this solecism, this anomaly, and substitute a system of direct taxation, equitably assessed, cheaply collected, and equally imposed, leaving commerce as free as the air we breathe, and restraining that governmental extravagance which, as Mr. Bright said, every government in its turn condemns, and none seems able to reduce.

III.

THE INCIDENCE OF TAXATION.

Probably no subject has given rise to more crotchets than that of the Incidence of Taxation. So long ago as 1690, the great John Locke maintained that, levy a tax how you will, it ultimately falls upon the land. "The merchant will not bear it," he says, "the labourer cannot, and therefore the landholder must." He then pertinently asks the landowner whether he had not better bear it "by laying it directly where it will at last settle, or by letting it come to him by the sinking of his rents, which, when they are once fallen, every one knows are not easily raised again." This great thinker has had numerous followers, and there are still many persons who believe in his doctrine. Others say that the cultivators of the soil recoup themselves by paying less wages, and that therefore any tax falls upon the labourer; others maintain that it falls upon profits, others again upon capital; while it is also argued, with great plausibility, that a tax, however levied, acts and reacts between labour and capital and land, until it has the very peculiar incidence of falling nowhere at all in particular, but diffusing itself among the entire population; that is to say that it has no fixed incidence. However originally levied, say these economists, it moves for ever, and never finally reaches a resting place, and says, "thus far will I go and no further."

It seems to me, however, that though interesting as samples of politico-economical puzzles, these speculations are of little practical moment. The question to be considered is, Who makes the sacrifice of a certain portion of his means in payment for the protection he receives from the government of his country? There is a great misconception on the subject. A great many persons think the poor pay no taxes whatever; others think they pay very little, and that in any readjustment of taxation they ought to be more heavily taxed. I can only account for such a misconception by concluding that the middle class forget all about indirect taxation. They forget they pay such taxes themselves, and it never occurs to them that the poorer classes are thus reached. They measure their payments to the State by the receipts for Income Tax and Inhabited House Duty, which they can see on their files, and knowing that few of the labouring classes pay taxes of that description, they imagine that their poorer brethren are altogether exempt. I trust, therefore, I am not departing from the subject under discussion, in pointing out that the working classes of this country are paying much more than their share, and that the remark of Mr. Gladstone, that the working men pay more in proportion to their incomes than the proudest nobleman in the land, is almost as applicable now as when it was uttered in 1866.

Mill argues, with very great force — and, indeed, it is now admitted — that the just incidence of taxation should be in obedience to the rule, that each subject in the State ought to make an equal sacrifice. This is what is called "the equality of taxation," and it is defined as meaning that the contribution of each person towards the expenses of government should be so apportioned, "that he shall feel neither more nor less inconvenience from his share of the payment than every other person experiences from his." If a person be overburdened by taxation, then some one is escaping his fair share; and of course, if one man is unjustly spared, then another is unjustly oppressed. If, therefore, it can be shown that the working classes are paying more than their share, then the wealthy classes are paying less than theirs.

Mr. Dudley Baxter, the eminent Conservative statistician, estimates that the manual labour class in the United Kingdom consists of twenty-three millions of persons, and the upper and middle classes of seven millions, the income of the former being £324,000,000 sterling, and that of the latter £489,474,000. Now the principal Imperial taxes paid by the manual labour class are Customs and Excise, of which it is probable it pays an equal share per head to that paid by the other classes, because, as Mr. Bright pointed out, twenty men sitting at one table will eat and drink about the same quantity as twenty men sitting at another table, though of course the quality of the viands may be different, as one twenty may be worth nothing at all, the other twenty may be millionaires. The manual labour class, therefore, contributes £33,000,000 sterling. " Assuming that the remaining ten millions of Customs and Excise, and the whole of the other Imperial taxes, amounting to twenty-two millions, are contributed by the upper and middle classes, [which is assuming a great deal,] they will pay, as their share of the public revenue, £32,000,000 sterling. It thus appears that the upper and middle classes, with an income of

£489,474,000, pay £32,000,000, and that the manual labour class, with an income of £324,625,000, pays £33,000,000; in other words, that the former pay 6½ per cent. on their income, and the latter 10 per cent. on their income. The due share of the manual labour class, if it contributed in proportion to its income, would be £25,000,000, or £8,000,000 less than the sum which it now pays. To this class, therefore, the concession of a 'free breakfast table' would be a simple act of justice."

The matter was put still more strongly by Sir Charles Dilke, in his speech to his constituents, in January, 1873. He then pointed out, that as Bentham proposed and Mill advocated " a certain minimum of income, sufficient to provide the necessaries of life to a moderately numerous family, should not be heavily taxed, but only the surplus beyond this. Suppose this minimum to be £50 a year for each family, and supposing the workmen to be five millions of families (which is not much above the mark), this would give £250,000,000 for necessaries. But their whole income is computed at £325,000,000 by Mr. Dudley Baxter, leaving only £75,000,000 of superfluities, which on this principle would be taxed; on this sum, £30,000,000 of taxes are raised. The rich are two millions of families, which gives £100,000,000 for necessaries; but they have £500,000,000, leaving £400,000,000 to be taxed, which bears little more than £50,000,000 of taxes."

These statements show not only that the working classes are at present unduly taxed, but also, it must be acknowledged, that under the present system, if duties of Customs and Excise were abolished, they would almost entirely escape taxation. But no free-trader proposes to abolish indirect taxation, unless a complete and just system of direct taxation can be substituted. What that substitute should be I hope to have an opportunity to suggest; and this much I here premise, that it is certain that no scheme can be accepted which does not reach the working classes in their fair and proper proportion. And I will say of the working men — and I think that having been brought up amongst them I am entitled to speak for them — that they do not wish to shirk their share of the national burdens. They complain now, not so much that they are overtaxed—they hardly know it—but that the taxes are obtained from them in a sly and surreptitious manner.

It is a mistaken notion that working men prefer to pay their taxes indirectly in sugar, tea, and beer, and that they would rebel against paying the tax-collector in hard cash. Such an assertion is a libel upon the intelligence of the British workman. Ever since working men have learned to ask for anything, they have asked for direct taxation. In almost every manifesto they issue, at almost every public meeting they address, at every election, their cry is for direct taxation; and believing as they do, that the wealthy oppose it to save their own pockets, it is one of those causes of social discontent which do so much to set class against class. True, in addition to the very poor, there is a small section of the working class who now pay through their breakfasts, their beer, and their tobacco, who would escape a direct tax, but they are those whose occupations take them from town to town, whose wages though high are precarious, and for whom no town can offer sufficient inducements to make it their permanent residence. These would be free from taxation, and I would much prefer that they should go free than that in order to reach them the whole of their fellow-workmen should be unduly taxed. It is foolish, however, to hope for any justice from a system of taxation which taxes the choice tobacco of the wealthy man to the extent of only 8 per cent. upon the dearest, and the tobacco of the poor to the extent of between 400 and 800, and even up to 1800 per cent. upon the cheapest, and which, while it admits free the pine-apples, grapes, and almonds of the wealthy, taxes the raisins, currants, and figs of the poor. In fact, all things considered, it is no exaggeration to say that the working classes pay twice as much per cent. on their incomes as do the rich upon theirs; and there is this injustice also to be borne in mind, that they contribute chiefly through necessaries, while the wealthy contribute through superfluities, the former contributing 96 per cent. of their taxes from the necessaries of life, while the wealthy only contribute 42 per cent. from that source. Indeed, it has been carefully calculated and published by the Council of the Financial Reform Association, that, whilst the payment of Customs and Excise duties may absorb one-fourth of the earnings of the working man with a family, the rich man, besides the privilege of getting his tea, coffee, sugar, etc., wholesale out of bond, thus paying no more than the Government receives, may contribute in this way less than a thousandth or a ten-thousandth part of his annual income.

There are other ways of showing the same irregularity. For instance, in 1872, the Secretary of the Rawtenstall Co-operative Stores pointed out that upon the six articles, malt, sugar, coffee, tea, and currants, sold from their stores, there was paid to the Revenue £1 5s. 10¼d. per man. All of them were working-men; and a similar calculation, made some years ago by three other co-operative stores, fully proves the incidence to be as stated by Mr. Dudley Baxter.

I have prepared two tables on this subject, to which I invite your attention. The first one shows the expenditure of a labouring man, whose family, including himself and wife and children, consists of five members. [See next page.] I have not selected a drunkard, nor have I chosen a teetotaller, but one whose expenditure on excisable articles is such as is met with in the majority of cases. It will there be seen that the commodities enumerated, which cost the labourer 17s. 6d., could have been bought for 15s. 1½d. had no indirect taxes been imposed. Now, the addition of 2s. 4½d. to 15s. 1½d. is equal to 15·702 per cent., and that is the rate of taxation to which the necessaries and comforts of life in use amongst the poor are subjected, independently altogether of the repressive influence which such taxation produces, by impeding the efforts of industrial genius. The per centage of 15·702 on the commodities is equal to 11·875 on the whole income of 20s. a-week.

E

EXPENDITURE of a LABOURER, who receives 20s. a Week, and whose Family, including himself and Wife and Children, consists of Five Members.

ARTICLES USED.	Amounts. £ s. d.	Total Expenditure. £ s. d.	Items of Tax. £ s. d.	Amount of Taxation. £ s. d.
Flour and Meal	0 4 10			
Butter, 1 lb. at 1s.	0 1 0			
Beef, 2 lbs. at 8d.	0 1 4			
Bacon, 1 lb. at 7d.	0 0 7			
Harrings	0 0 3			
Starch, Soda, Pepper, Medicine, and Sundries	0 0 6			
Candles, Firewood, &c.	0 0 3			
Coal	0 2 6			
Soap, 1 lb. at 4d.	0 0 4	0 11 6		
Tea, ¼ lb. at 2s.	0 1 0		0 0 3	
Sugar, 4 lbs. at 2½d. per lb.	0 0 10		0 0 2	
Coffee, ¼ lb. at 1s.	0 0 6		0 0 1	
Ale, 4 quarts, at 5d. per quart	0 1 8		0 0 2	
Tobacco, ¼ lb. at 4s. per lb.	0 1 0		0 0 9¼	
Spirits	0 1 0	0 6 2	0 0 3	0 1 8¼
Rent		0 0 6		
Balance remaining on hand, to provide Shoes, Hats, and other necessaries for himself and family		0 0 6		0 0 8
		1 0 0		0 2 4½

To this we have to add the Mercantile Profit on the 1s. 8¼d., the amount of duties advanced by the Merchant and Manufacturer, and the cost of collection .. ..

Again, deducting the money spent for the telegraphic and postal services, the expenditure for governing this country amounted, last year, to £2 1s. 5d. per head of the estimated population. But what does our poor labourer pay? Why no less than £6 1s. 4d., or nearly three times as much as the average. The man, therefore, who ought in common fairness to pay so much less than the average, we find contributing a very great deal more. It is no answer that he can avoid the taxes on luxuries. I have dealt with that question before. That is a question for him, not for us.

We come now to the second table, which is the expenditure of a middle-class family, of the same number as the labourer's, but which is in receipt of £5 a-week. [See next page.] Here we find that what cost £1 9s. 3d. might, but for taxes, have been obtained for 18s. 1d., which is a tax of 61·751 per cent. on the cost of the commodity. But he also pays 1·27 in direct taxes, and these are together equal to 12½ per cent. on his income.

Now, a similar table, giving the expenditure of a man with £1,000 a-week, would show that he would pay £17 10s. 7d. a-week in indirect taxes, and about £18 3s. in direct taxes, making a total of £35 13s. 7d., or only 3·568 per cent. on his income.

EXPENDITURE of a MIDDLE CLASS MAN, who is in the receipt of £5 a Week, and whose Family, including himself and Wife and Children, consists of Five Members.

ARTICLES USED.	Amounts.			Total Expenditure.			Items of Tax.			Total of Tax.		
	£	s.	d.	£	s.	d.	£	s.	d.	£	s.	d.
Tea, ¼ lb. per week at 3s. per lb.	0	1	6				0	0	3			
Sugar, 4 lbs. per week, at 3½d. per lb.	0	1	2				0	0	2			
Do., 2 lbs. " at 4½d. "	0	0	9				0	0	1½			
Coffee, Cocoa, &c., 1 lb. per week, at 1s. 6d. per lb.	0	1	6				0	0	2			
Porter and Ale	0	7	0				0	2	2			
Spirits	0	5	0				0	1	6			
Wine	0	5	0				0	0	9			
Preserved Fruits, Raisins, Prunes, Nuts, Currants, Figs, Almonds, &c.	0	2	6				0	0	1			
Tobacco and Cigars	0	4	10				0	3	3½			
Total per week				1	9	3						
Income Tax				0	0	9½						
Inhabited House Duty				0	0	4½				0	8	6
Average Expense for Cab, Hackney-coach, and Omnibus, and Railway				1	10	5						
Domestic Servant				0	7	0						
Other Expenditure with the Butcher, Baker, Tailor, Milliner, Shoemaker, Hatter, Ironmonger, Haberdasher, Linendraper, Coals, &c., &c.				0	4	0						
				1	10	2						
Rent of House and Rates				0	13	2						
Schooling, Sundries				0	15	3				0	2	8
				5	0	0				0	12	4

To this we have to add the Mercantile Profit on the 8s. 6d., the amount of duties advanced by the merchant and manufacturer, and the expense of Collection .. ..

Here, then, we have shown a striking anomaly of the present system of taxation, as shown by the unequal amount of taxation paid upon the same amount of income in the possession of different classes of persons.

1 Wealthy Person who enjoys a weekly Revenue from the Operations of Trade or the Employment of Money out of } £1,000 pays in Taxes, £35 13 7

200 Middle Class Men who collectively have a similar Amount of Income from Professional or other exertion out of .. .. .. } £1,000, pay in Taxes, £123 6 8

1000 Labourers whose weekly Earnings amount to .. } £1,000, pay in Taxes, £118 15 0

So that we find that while the lowest and the middle classes bear the burdens of taxation, those whose incomes are princely escape a great deal of the taxes which ought in justice to be borne by them. I hope, therefore, we shall hear no more about the working classes not paying their share of the taxes. If the wealthy classes were taxed in the same proportion to their means as the daily labourer and the middle-class man are to their means, and if all went into the Exchequer, the requirements of the State, even on the present extravagant scale, would be amply provided for, and, as Mr. Paton, of Montrose, has shown, the surplus would suffice to pay off our enormous National Debt, in the course of from a dozen to fifteen years.

Some people cry out that taxation and representation ought to go together. I would warn such people not to lay too much stress upon that point, because the working-classes of this country *all* pay taxes, and ought on that theory to have the votes which are now withheld from them.

There is a very common fallacy,—indeed Mr. Dudley Baxter has fallen into it,—which I should not like to pass unnoticed, and that is, that in large households the master of the house pays the taxes of the servants because he pays the grocer's bill. It must be remembered that there are two ways of paying servants: either a salary and board, or a larger salary without board. It is therefore at once seen that the amount deducted, so to speak, when the servants are boarded, is part of their wages, and as it is spent at the grocer's on their behalf, they, and not their employers, pay the tax. When a family goes on the continent and shuts up its town house, the servants are then put on "board wages," thus proving beyond a doubt that, although they may not "go shopping," they as veritably pay for the commodities and pay the taxes when they are not on board wages equally as if they were. The tax, therefore, falls on to the servants not the masters. This must be taken into consideration where the expenditure of the middle class man in the Table just quoted is dealt with; and it will of course lessen the difference between the proportion of taxes he pays according to his means, and that which the labouring man pays according to his means. But even if there were anything in the objection I have answered — which there is not — it would not much improve the question, for, as was pointed out by a correspondent in the *Financial Reformer*, taking the income of the Marquis of Bute at £300,000 per annum, the Marquis would have to support seventeen thousand adult consumers of taxable articles before he would be paying the same proportion of indirect taxes as a man with 20s. a week.

I think, then, I have shown that the incidence of taxation at the present day presses most severely upon the middle and the working classes; and although there has been some improvement since the last few years, when Prof. Leone Levi, in 1860, estimated the proportions paid by the classes at 12 per cent. for the upper, $11\frac{1}{2}$ per cent. for the middle, and 14 per cent. for the labouring class; and although the remission of indirect taxation has been a benefit to the working class more than to any other, yet these benefits have been at the expense of the middle class rather than of the rich, and there can be no doubt that in any scheme of re-adjustment a great deal more of the taxation of the country ought to be borne by the wealthy class. In this respect, too, it is better to be charitable, and err on the right side than otherwise. The class which has levied the taxes has not always used the best language when speaking of those who have paid the taxes. The working man may not be a paragon of perfection, and he may not always speak in the choicest language of those above him. He probably remembers that they have dubbed him "thug," "dreg," and "scum;" he may not forget that even "residuum" can be twisted by men who are supposed to know Latin into a term of opprobrium; while, perhaps, he also recollects that even one who pretends to be a "working man's friend" has styled the class "the vile substratum." The poor fellow has had all that to put up with—as if poverty were a crime—and I therefore think, that if any leniency is to be shown at all in regard to taxation, it should be to those who hitherto have suffered so much and endured so long. It is infinitely better that the poor should pay too little and the rich too much, than, as at present, the rich too little and the poor too much. I would rather that the rich should be taxed to spare the poor, than the poor to excuse the rich. St. Paul says, "We that are strong ought to bear the infirmities of the weak, and not to please ourselves."

IV.

Free Trade.

Great and important as the question of taxation is, when considered in the light of raising in just proportions the sum necessary for carrying on the government of the State, yet there is a question of wider scope and deeper importance in the proposal to substitute a system of direct for that of indirect taxation. That question is the principle of Free Trade, which, as Douglas Jerrold says, "is a spell by which the world will yet be governed."

I am glad, therefore, that the petition before you states that "the policy inaugurated by Sir Robert Peel has proved so eminently beneficial as to warrant further progress in that direction, not stopping short, ultimately, of entire freedom of trade, and the substitution of direct for indirect taxation." What is meant by that prayer is, that every step in the direction of free trade has been a good thing for everybody, and therefore we ought to crown the edifice by removing all existing impediments, hindrances, and embarrassments. What is alone surprising is, that a great many members of Parliament, who ought to know better, and a great many newspaper writers and contributors to the reviews, are constantly speaking as if Free Trade were an accomplished fact. They are so intoxicated, so to speak, with the splendour of the results of Corn Law repeal, that they can conceive no higher heaven — no further advance in the same direction. They think they have achieved the Be all, End all, and that no more can or need be done. These gentlemen forget that above half the revenue is still raised by a system entirely opposed to free trade. Any one who imagines that free trade is an accomplished fact should endeavour to land a cargo of tobacco at Ipswich, or to have wine tested at Hartlepool; or to import tea at even any place except London ; or he should try to get his vessel to Worcester Bridge ; or to plant his waste acres with beet, with chicory, or with tobacco; or to brew or distil, or to roast coffee; and he will soon see that his house is anything but his castle, and that there are many products in which there is no such thing, at present, as *free* trade in England; and when there is not free trade in every trade, there is not perfect freedom in any.

Indeed, let it be borne in mind that so long as we have a single custom-house or exciseman, no trade is or can be free. To abolish the duties on some commodities is but to slacken the bonds of trades. None are free so long as any remain fettered. Mr. Gladstone pointed out this when proposing the abolition of the duty on soap. "It may," said the great financier, "be thought there is a wide interval between the premises and the conclusion, if I say, in order to extinguish the slave trade, repeal the soap tax. But at all events a connection of ideas more legitimate cannot well be imagined. The map would show how many are the rivers of the coast of Africa; those rivers may for the most part become depôts for the trade in palm oil. The quantities you may receive from that source are, it is stated, almost immeasurable. There lie the great materials for a trade which, if you can only relieve it from restraint, will show that the energy and capital of the country are as well entitled to carry the prize in this particular direction, as they show themselves to be in so many others." Some similar observations might be made in regard to every industry. No one can foresee where the advantages of perfect freedom end. As Mr. Cliffe Leslie wrote, "Liberty only can reveal the directions the development of commerce and industry are destined to take, and financial statesmanship consists mainly in permitting it to do so."

Let me still further illustrate this by a paragraph from the *Times* :—" A lady who buys one of Sir Titus Salt's alpaca dresses little thinks how much the world has been set in motion to enable her to do so. Messrs. Halling and Pearce, or Swan and Edgar, go to the London warehouse, London warehouse goes to the Bradford merchant, Bradford merchant goes to the dyer and finisher and to Titus Salt, who goes to Liverpool agent to bring his wool to Saltaire from South Australia ; and the shipper at Liverpool sets the Lairds and Napiers to construct his ship to go to Melbourne, where again the shipper at Australia toils to get the fleeces from the sheep farmers, who are employed by my lady's cousin who emigrated some twenty-five years ago, who has made his fortune and is now in the Legislative Council. And then to consider the multitude of forces at each stage of the business — how the fleece is sorted into some twelve or more lengths and kinds, some good for Titus Salt, and some good for Gott of Leeds, and others useless to either. The worsted useful for Bradford, and the wool useful for Leeds, are two very different things, although coming from the same sheep's back.

Iron and steel then come forward; and the Whitworths make tools, and the Platts make the machines; and the alpaca is spun, and woven, and dyed, and pressed, and sold through several hands, each of which collects his percentage for his labour and skill, until at last my lady buys it.". To tax any one of these processes is to obstruct all, and therefore to restrict every trade, even the grocer, the butcher, the baker, and the tailor.

It is seen, then, that the most obvious result of releasing an industry from the trammels which beset and harass it, is an increased consumption in the produce of that industry. The adoption of partial Free Trade in this country has trebled its foreign trade. I might show you this, but it would simply be displaying before you a huge mass of figures, which could not possibly impress the mind with the real nature of the circumstance. The fact, however, is beyond dispute. Before the abolition of the Corn Laws, the quantity of British goods exported amounted in value to £1 18s. 9d. per head of the population. The quantity of British goods we now export amounts to £8 1s. 0d. of the present population. Now, let me ask, what is the result of an increase in the consumption of any commodity — say tea? You know that in 1865 the duty on tea was reduced from 2s. 2¼d. a pound to 6d. a pound. The immediate effect of that reduction was a great falling of price, and a great increase in the consumption of tea. In 1849, when the duty was at the former figure, the annual consumption per head in the United Kingdom was 1·81 lb.; in 1865, when the duty was reduced, the yearly consumption rose to $3\frac{1}{4}$ lbs. per head; and last year the average consumption had risen to 4 lbs. a head. Now, of course, this means that a great many more families were able to regale themselves with tea than had previously been able to do so. All of you who appreciate and enjoy a good cup of tea will acknowledge that there is a great advantage in that. But an increased consumption of tea means much more than that. It signifies, in the first place, that more ships have been required to fetch the tea from China, to build which ships more men are required, and to man them more sailors are wanted. The ships require rigging, which is good for the rope-makers, and the sailcloth manufacturers, as well as several other industries. Then when the tea arrives here, it requires more warehouses and employs more warehousemen, as well as an additional number of carriers, both by rail and road, to distribute it over the country; it requires more paper to wrap it in parcels, more string to tie them with; and indeed it is difficult to imagine any industry whatever which does not receive some advantage from the increase in the consumption of this or any other article. Remember, also, that all these processes to which I have alluded are not confined to England, but it stimulates in a similar way the various trades in the distant land which cultivated the plant, and thus two nations mutually benefit each other, and feel that they have an interest in each other's prosperity. As the late Napoleon said, "The greater the riches and prosperity of a country, the more it contributes to the riches and prosperity of all other countries."

Let us, however, still pursue the theme, for I have not yet finished the argument. The tea is not sent here for nothing. We send out other commodities in exchange for it. The cotton fabrics from Lancashire, the woollen cloths from Yorkshire, hardware goods from Birmingham, and steel and iron manufactures from Sheffield, are gathered to our ports, and sent to the East, employing labour at every process, and whenever they are moved, from the time the raw material is landed on our shores, until the time that it is delivered over to the consumer or the wearer in a distant land. An increase in the consumption of a commodity, therefore, gives work to thousands of men who would otherwise be idle; and when men are earning money they spend it. They buy more furniture for their homes, more clothes for their back, more and better food; and it is only when they are out of work, and as poor as Christopher Sly, that, like him, they have "no more doublets than backs, no more stockings than legs, nor no more shoes than feet." The prosperity of the working man, then, increases the prosperity of the butcher, the baker, the publican, the tailor, and all the manufactures and industries upon which these trades depend. To tax one is to restrict the trade in all. It is therefore evident that an increase in the consumption of any single commodity affects, and beneficially affects, the whole of the labour market, from one end to the other.

Now, as we cannot restrict one trade without all trades suffering, so we cannot have free trade so long as any single trade is trammelled, and no scheme could be more cunningly devised for restricting and annoying trade than our Custom House system. As procrastination is the thief of time, so rapidity in despatch is the very life and soul of modern commercial enterprise. Every delay increases the cost of a commodity; every additional person employed in its production or movements increases the cost, and it is

F

therefore essential that there should be as few causes as possible for the one, and as little necessity as possible for the other. I have pointed out on a previous occasion the extraordinary and farcical operation of the Custom House system. And yet such a state of things is inseparable from anything less than perfect freedom of trade. It is one of the anomalous results that must inevitably follow Custom House management wherever these institutions exist. Great Britain has, in fact, only sixteen ports and landing towns at which it is really worth her while to collect duties. But all the other ports must be watched at enormous expense, in order that the present system may be carried on.

Let me say a few words about this system of Customs and Excise. It is deeply to be regretted that the public do not know more than they do of these twin-horrors. The reason is that Parliament is not inclined to talk much about them. "It is not," says Mr. Leslie, whose admirable essay on Financial Reform you ought all to read, "the policy of Finance Ministers to find fault with taxes so long as it is convenient to retain them." In the first place, the army of Custom House officers in the United Kingdom nearly reaches the number of 6,000, exclusive of that part of the Coastguard Service employed in the protection of the revenue, and which amounts to about the same number. These form a *cordon* around our coast, preventing trade being carried on at any except licensed ports, and thus, it may be observed at the outset, preventing many a fishing village from developing into a thriving seaport town. Nature and the requirements of trade would naturally select the most appropriate spots whence to trade; but Her Majesty's Commissioners of Customs arrogate to themselves greater wisdom than the former, and have very little respect for the latter. They have, therefore, as I pointed out on another occasion, limited to certain places the exercise of the universal right to trade, both by importing and exporting also, although, as there are no duties levied whatever on exports, one would have thought that merchandise might have been allowed to leave England without let or hindrance from the most convenient places that could be found.

Any goods, whether imported or exported, may be weighed, searched, unpacked, repacked, and a whole host of other things done to them besides. The number of authorised places where any or all of these things can be done is, as already stated, 133; and at no other place, however well adapted it may be for an export or an import trade, can ships load their cargoes and merchants buy them. It is seen therefore that, when a ship is approaching this country, the price of its cargo to the community may be increased by its not being allowed to make for the nearest safe port, but by its being obliged to conform to these Customs regulations. It may, however, be thought that 133 is a sufficient number of inlets or outlets to satisfy the wants of the trading community. It is therefore well to remember that trading cannot be freely carried on at even all these ports. The right of importing wine, for instance, is limited to 59 of them, and wine imported into any other is forfeited. The wine trade, too, is subject to a still further restriction respecting the ports at which wine can be tested for duty, of which there are only eleven in the kingdom. The importation of tobacco, again, is limited to 35 of the 133 authorised ports, and it is only recently that so many as are now allowed to do so have been permitted to import tea; and the privilege is so hampered with restrictions as to be almost useless in every port except London.

There are, it is seen, three sorts of places around our coast. 1st. Those at which no importation or exportation whatever can take place. 2nd. Places at which goods generally can be imported and exported, but where the importation of some classes is forbidden, and of others impeded: and 3rd. Those which are permitted both to import and export under certain conditions. Now, one would have thought that in the selection of Custom House officials the Commissioners at any rate would have selected men who had some means of knowing the circumstances and capacities of each creek, bay, and estuary around the coast. On the other hand, the fact is, the men who have been selected to carry out the Custom House system, from the Chief Commissioner downwards, seem to have been chosen because they were inspired with a notion that it was their special function to restrict trade as much as possible. It is not surprising, therefore, to find that when the inhabitants of certain places have seen the advantage of their towns being made into ports, and have applied for that privilege, the request has been flatly refused. This is no rare thing, but has often taken place. An instance occurs to me.

A short time ago I was at Worcester, and as I stood on the graceful bridge which spans the Severn there, I could not help wondering how it was that a river so adapted for navigation, should loiter lazily along and waste itself in the ocean. I was struck also at a quay with the rusty railway lines half buried in the dust drift, and wondered why they had ever been laid, if instead of the busy traffic which one would have thought had called for them, there was no further use for the quay and its lines than to serve as a promenade for two nurse girls with perambulators, and two idlers with short clay pipes. It seems that the inhabitants of Worcester were, some time ago, actuated by the very natural desire of increasing the wealth of the town. With that view, a large sum of money— no less than a quarter of a million sterling—was spent in rendering the river Severn navigable as far as Worcester, in making the quay and the railway lines, preparing bonding warehouses, and doing all they could to make the dull old cathedral city into a lively port. Ships of 160 tons burthen, larger than that in which Columbus discovered America, could be brought up to the bridge, and had even taken—illegally, I suppose, as permission had not been given for their owners to trade—cargoes to the Mediterranean. The effect of Worcester being a port would be that Birmingham, Worcester, Kidderminster, and other large towns in the neighbourhood would all be brought, as it were, thirty miles nearer the sea, and any commercial man knows the advantage of that. There could be no doubt that the result would be a very large increase in the iron, earthenware, and other trades.

Such was the hopeful future which seemed to dawn upon the people of Worcester. Blessed, however, is he who expects nothing, for he shall not be disappointed. The authorities said in effect to a deputation on the subject, "We admit that you have completely made out your case. We believe that, as you say, there would be a very considerable trade; but to permit vessels to go thirty miles up a narrow river would lead to so much smuggling, and would require such an expensive establishment to prevent it, that it cannot be allowed." So this explains the desolation visible from the bridge at Worcester. Our system creates smuggling; but because there would be smuggling, you shall not have the advantage of our system. Strange logic! The quay might be busy with men collecting and distributing the products of a thousand industries. The quay is deserted. Magnificent warehouses might take the place of the present humble buildings, and the river might be crowded with ships, instead of lazily wasting itself in the ocean. Because, however, it is necessary to levy Customs duties, the quarter of a million was thrown away, a large and populous district is forbidden direct communication with the sea, and all is lost that was done with so much care, labour, and expense.

The people of Worcester and its district, including such towns as Birmingham, Wolverhampton, and Droitwich, are at a disadvantage as compared with other places, and have not only to pay an extra tax in the way of increased cost of land carriage, but they are deprived of a large foreign trade. This is all the more galling, because other places with not half the claims of Worcester have been made ports, and avail themselves so little of the privilege that they do not even collect the expenses of the Custom House; and others, although honoured with large Custom House establishments, do not collect a single penny. Verily Worcester —with the brand on its forehead of being forbidden to trade—is in itself an energetic protest against the iniquitous system of indirect taxation, which at present deprives the country of the advantage of free trade.

I do not know how to give you an adequate notion of the inconveniences, and therefore losses, attendant on our Custom House system. I could weary you with instances. I was reading the other day the *Customs Officers' Manual*, which, amongst other things, startled me with the information that, though tea may be legally admitted into many of the ports in the United

Kingdom, yet the restrictions are so exacting that the importation of that commodity is virtually confined to London, while Hartlepool, Lynn, Ipswich, Greenock, Newcastle, and other places, are not considered fit places for its reception; so that I suppose if a vessel arrives in Newcastle with a cargo for that town, part of which is tea, it must land all but that, and then proceed to London with the tea. The instructions to the officers in the book I have mentioned, shewing how they have to board, to rummage, to seal up the exciseable stores in the ship, and to examine them every day, and a host of other things, take up twenty-two pages, while instructions as to warehousing, etc., nearly all of them of an absurdly intricate character, occupy other twenty-seven pages. The process of delay a commodity is subjected to in the warehouse is remarkable. A writer, in the *Produce Markets Review*, has calculated that if the various forms which have to be filled up whenever any commodity arrives in England were pasted together, they would form a carpet 29 feet $9\frac{1}{2}$ inches long, by 28 feet 2 inches wide. These forms are thirty-eight in number, and of course require a great number of clerks to work at them, who might be more productively employed. I have read letters upon letters detailing the inconvenience, expense, absurdity, and waste attending taxed articles, even in the bonding warehouses. To illustrate the kind of annoyances to which merchants are subjected by the obnoxious system of Custom Houses, I will give an extract from a letter from a firm of Liverpool shipbrokers with which I am acquainted, written to one of their foreign clients. The letter is dated 16th August, 1873, and the extract is as follows:—"Delay has been caused entirely by vexatious Customs regulations, which we had never previously come into contact with, or even heard of. We mentioned in our last that we had obtained permission to draw off the spirit into tins as required, but we found at last that this by no means included permission to mix medicines or perfumery with it, and this we were flatly refused. However, we found that in London, though not in Liverpool, perfumery might be mixed with spirit, and accordingly you may expect the Ess. Rosæ, Geranii, Menth., Pip., and Alkanet by the first steamer next month; but the other articles we are not allowed to prepare in this free country, and therefore cannot send. We must say we feel mortified and ashamed that such stupid restrictions upon trade should still exist in England at this time—but we cannot overcome them. If you would like the medicines and spirit separately we can send them without difficulty; but we suppose our Customs authorities have discovered that mixing is a crime and misdemeanour."

Sometimes, too, the departments get at loggerheads. Not long ago, a firm imported 300 pipes of wine, and, for a good reason, bonded half of them in the Custom House vaults, the other half in those of the Inland Revenue. Subsequently, the merchant had an order for 200 pipes. He got the 150 from the Custom House, but on application to the Inland Revenue for 50 from the other lot, he was refused, and the Customs authority he showed was laughed at by the Inland Revenue officers; and to such a pass did the quarrel between the two Government departments get, that after great delay and inconvenience the Customs officials broke open the doors of the warehouse of the others, and the 50 casks required were obtained by force.

I must not weary you by pursuing this uninteresting phase of the question. No description or mere recital of instances can convey an adequate idea of the inconvenience and annoyance to the trades concerned, of the vast amount of corruption the system gives rise to, and of the loss to the public. Every trade is harassed, and every commodity which gets into the claws of the

Custom House, becomes so much dearer to the consumer. I conclude by calling attention to what is called "racking." Racking, I believe, is the pumping of spirits from one cask into another, or the filling of a number of small casks from a large one. Until recently, I am told, this was done either by the distiller or the retailer, free from Excise intermeddling, and therefore without any cost to the public; whereas racking in warehouse is now performed under Excise supervision at the public expense. Books and forms are prepared in London and distributed over the kingdom, not for the public use, but for that of private traders; and the time of public-paid servants is largely occupied in attendance on processes in which the public have not the slightest interest or concern. In this racking business any deficiency not exceeding 1 per cent. is to be disregarded; yet 1 per cent. of the spirit duty amounts to £110,000 annually; no small sum to be thrown away, just that publicans and others may be saved the trouble of sorting their own spirits, and which sum, if "racking" were not done by public servants, would of course find its way into the exchequer.

Although the bonding system somewhat alleviates the evils I have mentioned, yet the wine trade complains that the saving is very little; and competent judges show that if the bonding system were abolished, 10 per cent. would be saved; while from "loss in warehouse" another 5 per cent. are sacrificed, and by gauging, 10 per cent., making a total loss of 25 per cent. "at the very least." As a large importer says: "It may possibly be said that these interruptions and impediments of Customs regulations are trifling and insignificant, or, at least, of no great importance; but in commerce, no check, however apparently slight in itself, can be disregarded as insignificant in effect. Fetters, however slight, are still fetters, and must more or less impede progress. As in some mighty engine, the intrusion of the smallest particle of a foreign substance into its machinery causes immediate derangement or suspension of its action, and, if not promptly removed, might eventually cause its destruction. So in commerce. An accumulation of petty impediments, with 'damnable iteration,' may at last, like the threads that bound Gulliver, prove sufficient to paralyse even the most healthy and persistent vitality." To all these annoyances have to be added the fact that shippers have to employ clerks on purpose to attend to Custom House business, which of course is an additional item in the cost of commodities.

I think, then, that I have shown that the system of

Customs and Excise is really a blockade of our own coasts, rivers, and harbours against free intercourse with all the nations of the earth. Custom House duties impede the exchange of commodities with foreign countries. Their collection necessitates numerous and expensive buildings, warehouses, revenue cutters and cruisers, and innumerable Government officials; and the abolition of the whole system would not only cause much less money to be required to pay for the collection of the revenue, thus reducing the national burdens, but would materially increase the ability of every subject to bear his share of those burdens.

Gentlemen, if Free Trade be not a good thing, let us sacrifice what we have of it and go back to protection. Ought commodities to be taxed? Then go to Middlesborough or Barrow-in-Furness and advocate a duty on the manufacture of Iron. Go into Lancashire and propose a duty on cotton. Go to Yorkshire and suggest a tax upon Australian wools. Why the whole British army could not carry out such a policy. People would see that the withdrawal of so much capital from the workshops would be followed by less work, and a great many of the artizans now in full employment would soon be clamouring round the doors of the workhouse. On the other hand, it has been

FREE TRADE.

stated, by a competent authority, that were customs and excise abolished, we should be able to buy for ninepence that for which we now have to give a shilling. It will at once be seen that this is no exaggeration, because when a person now spends one shilling at the grocer's for cocoa, $1\frac{3}{4}$d. is for the Government; out of one shilling's worth of coffee, $2\frac{1}{4}$d. is for the State; out of one shilling's worth of currants, $3\frac{5}{8}$d.; raisins, $2\frac{1}{8}$d.; tea, $4\frac{1}{4}$d. Why need I suppose a case? Did not Mr. Lowe attempt a retrograde policy by his insane proposal to impose a duty on matches? He failed to see the restrictions which such a tax would impose upon other industries than match making: the manufacturing chemist, the timber trade, the printing trade, the paper trade, and I know not how many others. It is no argument to answer, It was to be a small duty. The annoyance and the expense are the same, whether the duty be great or small. Look at the case of America. The imposition of duties has ruined the ship-building trade in America. In six years that trade fell off one-half. In 1860, no fewer than fifteen thousand men were employed in New York in building and repairing marine steam engines. In 1870, fewer than seven hundred found employment in the same branch of industry. You will be surprised to hear, that in the opinion of the Hon. D. Kelly, late president of the

American Institute of Mining Engineers at Philadelphia, the effect of what free trade we have in England has been to foster anarchy in Ireland, and to rob the life of the labourer in England and Scotland of all its joys. "The millions of sturdy men" declared this paragon of a politician "represented by Bradlaugh, Odger, Joseph Arch, and the travelled and humane patrician, Sir Charles Dilke, know that the world owes every man a living, and that it is only by protection that the means of living can be secured to the people."

The Hon. David Wells, the Cobden of America, has recently pointed out to Englishmen the great evils that have fallen upon his country in consequence of its blind and foolish policy. His terse eloquence is so convincing that I make no apology for quoting largely from his speech. He tells us that the present American tariff has produced nothing but "disaster and failure." Wages have not increased in the same proportion as in Europe; the purchasing power of the dollar is less than ever it was. Exports were never less, and imports never dearer. "The flag of the American commercial marine has been almost swept from the ocean." When the Shah visited Liverpool there was only one ship which could float the Stars and Stripes; while, I have been informed by a

Liverpool shipper, that a few years ago, American vessels were "fashionable," so to speak, and were preferred to the English ships, but that now American ships cannot be found. "There was exhibited," said Mr. Wells, " at Vienna last summer, one of the recent wonders of American invention; namely, a model of a Yankee shoe factory, in which all the work essential for the making of a shoe—the cutting, pegging, sewing, shaping, heeling, and polishing—are performed by machinery, and in which one man is enabled to do in greater perfection the work formerly performed by two; and yet, more surprising than all, is the fact that, notwithstanding this machinery has come into general use, boots and shoes in the United States now cost fifty per cent. more than they did prior to its invention, and our export trade in these commodities, which was formerly large, has become very inconsiderable."

Perhaps the climax of Anti-Free Trade principles is shown in the following extract:—" In short, the whole aim and object of this school of economists has been to engraft upon the country a sort of Chinese policy of prohibition and exclusion; and their great leader and teacher, Henry C. Carey, of Philadelphia, has not hesitated to publicly express his opinion that the very best thing which could happen to the United States would be to have the ocean that rolls between the two continents converted into a sea of fire so impassable, that if Dives was in Europe and Lazarus in Pennsylvania, they could not under any circumstances enter into commercial correspondence. And within a comparatively recent period, also, this same individual, who, it will be remembered, aspires to the reputation of a great teacher, has over and over again expressed the opinion that the death of Richard Cobden was one of the crowning mercies for which the United States had cause for gratitude; for the reason that if Mr. Cobden had lived, it was his purpose to have again visited America, and that such was the universal respect of the people for his name and his services, that they would in crowds have flocked to his speaking, a contingency especially to be dreaded, lest in hearing with their ears, and understanding with their hearts, they should have become converted to his principles."

There is, however, still some hope for that great nation. The shoe is beginning to pinch. The woollen manufacturers, the agriculturists, and the steel manufacturers are crying out. "The mills of the gods," said Mr. Wells, "though grinding exceedingly slow, nevertheless grind sure and fine, and the time now draws near when the judgment of the American people, long delayed, is likely to be so manifested in opposition to the doctrine of protection, as to cause it to disappear for ever, as an element, from the fiscal policy of the Government. But this result, when it occurs, will not be due so much to argument or individual effort as to the force of circumstances, which are compelling thought and conviction amongst the masses, whether they will it or no. Thus, within the past two years, the United States, as you all well know, have been visited by two remarkable and terrible conflagrations—the one in Chicago and the other in Boston. The first impulse in both cases, as soon as the people recovered from the shock of their disaster, was to petition for a removal of the tariff on the import of those articles necessary for a reconstruction of their habitations and places of business; thus unconsciously testifying that the general result of protection was diminution of abundance—a premium on scarcity and a restriction on growth, that in the time of calamity was scarcely endurable. The request in the first instance was acceded to on the part of Congress, but in the second refused—the protectionists becoming alarmed at the inevitable logic of the transaction; but the circumstance, nevertheless, occasioned not a few to ask themselves why a course of legislation that was acknowledged to be beneficial to those temporarily made destitute, was not likely to prove equally satisfactory to those made permanently poor by reason of other circumstances."

Again, gentlemen, I repeat that every step, however faltering that step may have been, which we have made towards free trade, has been beneficial. The history of the importation of every commodity proves this. No sooner was the duty off paper than a large import trade in rags set in. Before the duties were taken off timber, furniture being admitted duty free, English carpenters actually had to emigrate to make furniture for their own country, because it could be made cheaper abroad. Now, however, there is a great export trade from England. Ask anyone if it be desirable to re-impose the timber duties. What was the result of the French treaty, which it was prophesied would ruin Macclesfield and Coventry? Coventry and Macclesfield will tell you they have suffered nothing, but gained much. The increase of trade between England and France, which that treaty gave rise to, was enormous. The result was well pointed out by an American paper. "By exchange with England, France gets for eighty dollars in silks, cottons which would otherwise cost her ninety-six dollars,—a handsome gain of twenty per cent. England gets, for cottons costing a hundred dollars, silks which would otherwise have cost her a hundred and twenty dollars,—another handsome gain of twenty per cent." As soon as the treaty was ratified, the Bradford hotels filled with buyers from France, and firms in Manchester, Birmingham, London, Leeds, Sheffield, and other towns opened branch offices in Paris. Then, again, when the tea duty was reduced, I find from the *Times*, that India rejoiced with an exceeding great joy. "New tea companies, all sound, are springing up every day, and several coffee companies have been established in Madras. A gentlemen, who has just returned from a visit to Cachar, says the whole valley is now owned by English settlers, under Lord Canning's waste land rules. Savage Kookies, who used to cut each others throats, and those of our subjects, are now thriving labourers in neat cottages. A valley, destitute of population and worthless to the State before the mutiny, now yields a good revenue, besides the purchase-money of the land, and is as smiling as an English county." "Already," says Mr. John Noble, "two of our colonial possessions have established free trade with the best results. It has raised Singapore from the condition of a fishing village to that of a prosperous mart; while in the West, Vancouver's Island had followed the example, and in three years its imports of British goods rose from 458,511 to 2,000,000 dollars." Go back to protection, forsooth! Ask the British merchants. One more instance. Mr. Edmund Potter, ex-M.P. for Carlisle, in addressing his workpeople a short time ago, reminded them that when he started the calico printing works at Dinting Vale, in 1825, there was not a single article used in the works which was not taxed, whether it were timber, glass, soap, starch, salt, paper, cotton, madder dyes, or oil. It was, Mr. Potter says, very up-hill work in these days. "If," said he, "I were asked to what I owe my prosperity, I should say that it was based simply on the good free-trade measures which have been passed within the last forty years." I hope you will not think I have dealt too much in quotations. I have done so advisedly. I think it much better, when speaking of the influence of certain restrictions on trade, to select the testimony of those who are competent to speak of its influence, rather than give in my own words what could only be the opinion of an amateur. On such a subject, too, as the abstract question of Free Trade, I believe that my argument is strengthened by quoting the opinion of those whose authority is acknowledged, rather than give the same opinion without such authority.

Taxes on imports are virtually taxes on exports as well, by diminishing our demand for those commodities in which the foreigner pays us. They therefore limit the good which might otherwise be accomplished, and bring about the least good to the least number, instead of, like free trade, the greatest good to the greatest number. It must be remembered that no country can export an article or product to any extent unless it is prepared to sell the same as cheap as other nations; and therefore the ability or inability to export becomes a true test of the ability or inability, profitably, to produce for the domestic market. That is to say, that if foreigners will not buy of us, it is because we are charging too much for our commodities; and if we are doing that we are causing a loss to our own countrymen. It is no answer to say, It is no loss, because we never had them cheaper. I hold that where a man, or a nation, might have gained, and is prevented from doing so, he, or it, suffers a loss. A gentleman once drew my attention to the fact, that a printing-press had been purchased on the continent by one of the London newspaper proprietors, and my friend said, "See what free trade is doing; the foreigners are able to buy iron in this country, make it into machines in their own, and then bring it over here and undersell us in our own market." He thought that a sign that the country was going to pieces. I saw nothing alarming in the fact. The machine must have been able to do the same or a greater amount of work at a less cost than others they could buy here or it would not have been purchased, in which case capital was liberated for the employment of labour in other channels, while the machine itself caused more paper, more printing ink, et cetera, et cetera, to be used than were used before, and thus industries were stimulated and employment increased.

I mention this, because now-a-days we hear something of "Revivers of Industry" and others, who cry aloud for Reciprocity, and talk a deal about the Balance of Trade. I will not insult your intelligence by dwelling on such vagaries. When we buy more than we sell, we must be gainers. When we buy cheaper than we can produce, we are also gainers. Exportation represents labour, importation wealth. In fact, the exports cannot increase if the imports are restricted; and the answer, that when we change goods of different prices, one party must lose, is fallacious. It is the comparative, not the actual, value which must be looked to; and all that concerns us is the value to us. This was well put by the American paper I have just quoted.

What we have to do is to freely admit all the imports we can get. Take care of the imports, the exports will take care of themselves. The "balance of trade" and the "reciprocity" arguments have no weight with me. Mr. Bright clenched all such objections by asking, "If the foreigner refuses to buy cheaply of us, will it mend the matter if we refuse to buy cheaply of him?"

Of course, in speaking of free trade, I mean free trade in everything, including land and banking. These are, however, two phases of the question too elaborate in detail to be treated of on this occasion. The Bank Charter Act creates a monopoly and causes panics. The peculiar tenure of land creates a worse monopoly still. The Bank Charter Act has often to be suspended, and ought to be suspended altogether, while as to free trade in land I cannot do better than give its definition as in the words of John Bright: "It means the abolition of the law of primogeniture, and the limitation of the system of entails and settlements, so that, 'life interests' may be for the most part got rid of, and a real ownership substituted for them. It means also that it shall be as easy to buy or sell land as to buy or sell a ship, or, at least, as easy as it is in Australia, and in many or in all the States of the American

Union. It means that no legal encouragement shall be given to great estates and great farms, and that the natural forces of accumulation and dispersion shall have free play, as they have with regard to ships, and shares, and machinery, and stock-in-trade, and money. It means, too, that while the lawyer shall be well paid for his work, unnecessary work shall not be made for him, involving an enormous tax on all transactions in connection with the purchase and sale of lands and houses. A thorough reform in this matter would complete, with regard to land, the great work accomplished by the Anti-Corn Law League in 1846. It would give an endless renown to the Minister who made it, and would bless to an incalculable extent all classes connected with, and dependent on, honest industry."

Gentlemen, I have not laid before you the whole case of Free Trade. That was done thirty years ago by Mr. Cobden and Mr. Bright, and to the history of that time I must refer those who are not yet converts to its principles. All I have attempted is to draw your attention to a few of the arguments in its favour which seem to be forgotten to-day. There seems to be still a lingering after the Custom House and the exciseman. Have I not shown how they hinder commerce, restrict trade, cramp industries, and really tax labour? Commerce, Isaiah says, is a "holiness unto the Lord." Surely that should be remembered when it is proposed so to surround it with restrictions that its condition becomes one of thraldom and its results oppression. I might also show, that customs and excise interfere with and prevent inventions. "It is a well-known fact," wrote J. Stuart Mill, "that the branches of production in which fewest improvements are made are those with which the Revenue officer interferes." Probably, if coffee were introduced free, the English people would know how to prepare it. At any rate, the prevention of new discoveries is witholding comforts from the people. I might have pointed out many other things, but I hope you are already acquainted with them.

I trust I have shown that every duty is a spoliation of the masses for the profit of the producer; a robbery of the many for the benefit of the few; making the rich richer, and the poor poorer. It is sometimes said, "Tax luxuries only." It is true that luxuries are consumed by the rich, but their production employs thousands and thousands of the poor. Wine is the staple product of the whole of the South of Europe, and a population of from forty to fifty millions is more or less engaged in its production; a population, too, be it remembered, not of Asiatics, not of half-civilised and half-clothed people, but of like habits and of similar civilisation to our own, inhabiting also countries easily accessible to our ships, and consequently in every respect in a condition the most favourable to the trade of this country, and doubtless requiring many of its productions.

Free schools, free churches, free land may be wanted; but above all, free importation is wanted. Labour is not free so long as the fruit of labour is not. It is not enough that the farmer should be at liberty to grow what he likes, or the handicraftsman to make what he likes; they should be free to procure, in exchange for what they have produced, the utmost of all other things that they want. "Surely," as Mrs. Somerville once said, "as much food as a man can buy with as much wages as a man can get, for as much work as a man can do, is not more than the natural, inalienable birthright of every man whom God has created with strength to labour and with hands to work."

Sir Robert Peel, Cobden, and others have stated, over and over again, that if the principle of Free Trade be good for corn it is good for everything else; and Cobden added that, if any one have doubts as to whether indirect taxes obstruct commerce, impede manufactures, and check the production of wealth, he ought to compare the progress of a free port like Hamburg with a Custom House bound place like Havre. What does England now fear from bad harvests? She knows she may suffer from them, but she knows also she can bear the trial. The misery of the Corn Laws can never be repeated. We know that when we have bad harvests at home we can rely upon corn from distant regions whose very whereabouts as cornfields were never dreamed of during the time the Corn Laws were in existence, and would never have been thought of but for the stimulus to trade which the repeal of those laws gave. This is how it is with corn. England is becoming the corn mart of the world; she might be the same for sugar, and indeed, from her central position,* for all the commodities produced in every country on the face of the earth.

Gentlemen, although I have not mentioned the higher and nobler, the deeper and wider mission of Free Trade, I have not forgotten it. There is no

* "It is a fact," wrote Sir John Herschel, "not a little interesting to Englishmen, and, combined with our insular station in that great highway of nations, the Atlantic, not a little explanatory of our commercial eminence, that London occupies nearly the centre of the terrestrial hemisphere."

country now entirely independent of all others for everything it requires. Cosmopolitanism is day by day becoming a fact. Cobden said, "Free Trade is the International Law of the Almighty," and he spoke truly. He never spoke falsely. Why, then, not recognise the truth? Why encourage anomalies? To unite nations, on the one hand, with railways, telegraphs, and the general shortening of distances, and to separate them, on the other, by the establishment of artificial barriers, are two sorts of incompatible things, of which one ought and must necessarily destroy the other.

In the earliest stage of society, robbery and plunder were more honourable than labour—commerce was unknown. In the dark ages, nations only came into contact with each other sword in hand amid the din of war. Then it was thought that the prosperity of a nation depended upon the subjection in which it could keep its neighbours. Commerce is fast making all this obsolete. The "Rule Britannia, Britannia rules the sea" doctrine is giving place to the fraternal strife of industry. As Mr. Gladstone says, "It is not that one country extorts from another that which another reluctantly yields as the dictate of an imperious necessity; but that each freely and intelligently gives to each that which each can best afford, and for which it receives in return far more than the value." The removal of all obstructions to this intercourse would tend to the annihilation of national jealousies, prejudices, misunderstandings, and the other causes which have often led to actual warfare. No one can consider the various products of different climes without seeing that fair exchanges, to the benefit of all, may be made between the frigid North and the luxurious South, the wide prairies of the West and the looms of the East. No one can fail to see an identity of interests all over the world. However much the various nations of the earth may differ in manners and customs, however widely they may be separated in religion, whatever may be their language or their colour, there is one bond — Free Trade, unshackled industry — that binds them together with the golden clasps of brotherhood, and spreads from zone to zone, and from pole to pole, that goodwill among men which is the safest, the surest, and the best way of securing peace upon earth.

V.

THE NATIONAL EXPENDITURE.

In approaching the question of National Expenditure, a strong objection is met with at the very outset. It is said that it is impossible justly to criticise proposed reductions without a departmental knowledge of the offices to which those reductions refer; that no man is competent to speak of a less expenditure on our defensive forces without an intimate acquaintance with the innermost workings of the Admiralty, the Horse Guards, and the War Office; that we ought not to advocate the reduction of Ambassadors' salaries without having held the post of Foreign Secretary; nor object to the sinecural office of the Lord Privy Seal, unless we have been fortunate enough to have had a seat in the Cabinet.

There is considerable force in this objection. No man can fathom the workings of all the departments of the State, and no man is therefore competent to point out the exact places where reductions may be made. But, on the other hand, certain things come to light which make men stare with astonishment. If the various blunders, corrupt practices, and the expensive whims and oddities which are continually brought to the surface be an outward and visible sign of the hidden depths of incompetency, extravagance, and a reckless disregard for what is right and proper, which lie buried beneath the delicate politeness of officialism, then no one can be at a loss as to how and where great reductions in the national expenditure should be made.

It must be remembered, too, that those most likely to know the truth are day by day calling aloud for a reduced expenditure. Mr. Gladstone has called the expenditure "immoral," Mr. Bright has asked for an earnest public opinion to check that extravagance which every Ministry in turn condemns, and which none seems able to reduce; while the latter on the one hand, and Lord Derby on the other, as well as others who are competent to form a judgment, have fixed upon £10,000,000 as a minimum amount by which the national expenditure might be reduced. I take it, then, that there is no disputing that our expenditure is much too great, and the fact that an order-loving people like Englishmen — the most easily governed people on the face of the earth — should cost nearly £5 apiece per annum to be kept secure and in order, a cost greater than that of any other nation, is a disgrace upon those who rule us, and a sad reflection upon our character as a business nation.

Perhaps it would be as well at the outset to point out how it is that money is so easily granted for the Government to spend. Those who have been in the House of Commons when it has been in Committee of Supply must have looked upon the whole thing as a perfect farce. In the early hours in the morning about a dozen members—often less—lounge on the seats of the House of Commons. Some of them are yawning, others are sleeping; a few are chatting, while fewer still are paying any attention to the work of the Committee. The Chairman is rapidly gabbling something about thousands and hundreds of thousands, and in a very short time a few millions of John Bull's money have been ordered to be spent, either upon guns or pensions, or follies of one kind or another. When Sir John Pakington rose to continue the debate on Mr. Fowler's motion for the reduction of the army by ten thousand men, in the Session of 1872, there were present exactly ten stewards of the national purse; and the last time Mr. Goshen introduced his Navy Estimates, there were not forty members present. Perhaps

Mr. White, Mr. Dillwyn, Mr. Rylands, Mr. Mellor, or some other financial reformer opposes a certain vote. The chances are, he will be induced to withdraw his motion on account of some specious excuse which the Government has at hand. Occasionally, however, a division will be demanded, and as soon as the bells ring it is found that the "Whip" has sufficient members lounging about the smoke-room ready at any moment to form a majority, who come and vote they know not and they care not on what, and having voted in obedience to the command of the "Whip," they go back to their cigars and their billiards, sadly complaining of those "bores," the economists. Now, how is it that the "Whip" is enabled to have at his beck and call a small army of obstructives to economy? I will tell you, and when I have done so, I think you will acknowledge that there is something more than a mere illustration of apposite phrases in Cobbett's Grammar when it says, "House of Commons—Den of thieves."

A short time ago, I was told by the representative of one of the largest constituencies in this country, that if a member of Parliament would only support his party by his votes for a few years, through evil report and good report, whenever called upon to do so by the "Whip," he could then have as a reward for his obedience, a baronetcy if he wanted it, or an appointment, or a pension; or if he were above all that sort of thing, then some such favour could be shown to those of his friends whom he chose to select. This seemed to me so extraordinary that, although shortly afterwards it was repeated to me by an ex-M.P. who had had great experience in the House of Commons, yet I could hardly believe it. Nevertheless, I determined to see if I could learn anything further on the subject. The public utterances of members of Parliament soon satisfied me that my informants' statements were true. In April, 1873, Mr. Joshua Fielden, the Conservative member for the Eastern Division of the West Riding of Yorkshire, was addressing a portion of his constituents at Birstal, and speaking of the sum of money voted for the Civil Service, he characterised it as "that fund from which pensions were provided for those who sat and said nothing behind the Government, but who steadily voted for them"; and the very next month the same honourable member in the House of Commons itself moved the rejection of the Superannuation Act Amendment Bill, on the ground that it led to men being employed who were inefficient public servants, and because "when a Government was hardly pressed there was such an inducement to abolish old offices, to pension off the holders of them, and to create new ones for the hangers-on of the Government, that the system became most demoralising in its operation." These are the words of a Conservative member. Now I will give you the words of a supporter of Mr. Gladstone. In September, 1872, Mr. McCombie was addressing his supporters in West Aberdeenshire, and with great *naïveté* he spoke as follows: " I have had the pleasure of obtaining situations for some of my friends in West Aberdeenshire, but in some cases I have failed; but I trust no one will attribute my failure to any unwillingness on my part to oblige my constituents. When I say that there are over three hundred and fifty Liberal members in the House of Commons, all of them striving to obtain situations for their friends, and that one hundred of them may be applying for one situation, you will understand how difficult a task the Government have to perform in the distribution of their patronage. I have had no reason to complain, for I have had a very fair share of the patronage of the Government." Having thus given you the words of a Conservative and a Liberal, I will tell you what a Radical says. Sir Charles Dilke, in a speech at Glasgow, in September, 1872, said,

"I can name to you offices which are perfect sinecures, and to which fresh appointments have been made within a year, with a public statement to Parliament that there are duties to perform, and a private admission that such is not the case." When I stated the above facts at Kendal, in October, 1872, Mr. Whitwell, the member, gave a qualified confirmation of the fact, and indeed right and left, and all around, there is abundant evidence of this disgraceful state of things. I might give you much more evidence of a like nature. Professor Fawcett objects to the nationalisation of land, because amongst other things it would give more patronage to the Government, of which they have, he says, already too much; while Lord Derby makes a similar objection to the appropriation of railways by the State. Amongst the amenities of the Tichborne trial, is the answer of Mr. H. D. Seymour to the question, "What has become of Sir Edward Doughty's valet?" when the honourable member for Poole replied, "I got him a berth in the Customs,"— while the appointments that are made, no one knows how, the baronets that are created no one knows why, all tend to show a state of things at St. Stephens of which voters have little idea. The whole system is so permeated with all that is bad, that, as

Mr. Gladstone once said, nothing short of a revolution could sweep it away. We lift up our hands with pious horror when we hear of the Canadian Scandal and the Fisk frauds. It would be as well to look a little nearer home; and although Hosea Biglow's American senator, could sing,—

> A marciful Providunce hez fashioned us holler,
> O' purpose thet we might our principles swaller;

yet the British senator is not wholly exempt from the same sort of thing.*

Having, then, shown you the character of the stewards of the national purse, and pointed out the *modus operandi* of voting the supplies, you will hardly be surprised to hear that the State Departments show little beyond inefficiency, mismanagement, extravagance

---

* Both political parties are equally culpable in respect of these practices, and the following instance is given for no other reason than that it is of recent occurrence. A few years ago a certain gentleman, ambitious for a seat in the House of Commons, was proposed as a member of the Reform Club, but was blackballed. He at once turned Conservative, and as money was no object, a seat was soon found him. It is said that he has invented a successful mode of contesting elections, and that having spent £40,000 on behalf of the party he adopted, he is looked at as certainly a future baronet. He has been already rewarded with an office under the present Government. All his pleasure, however, is not unalloyed, as he has earned the *soubriquet* of "charlatan of the tory party," and it is humorously observed that he ought to be a "right honourable" as "First Commissioner of Dirty Works," with a seat in the cabinet.

and worse. The Audit Department cannot audit, and the result is, there is no such thing as a clear and intelligible National balance-sheet. If one thing more than another would open people's eyes to the truth of the matter, it would be the publication of an annual balance-sheet, such as our merchants and tradesmen could understand. The Government shrinks from such a task which, however, has been undertaken by Mr. Lloyd Morgan, of London, whose services the Financial Reform Association have been fortunately able to secure, and thus, in the Almanack of that Association, a clear and concise balance-sheet is always to be seen. Do not think I am exaggerating when I say that the Government accounts are in a muddle, such as the paltriest tradesman would be ashamed of, and such as would draw down on the head of a bankrupt the severest censure, if nothing worse, of the presiding judge.

One would think that in a commercial country like England, the system of book-keeping was the most perfect it was possible to conceive. Marvellous to relate, however, just the contrary is the fact, and the loose, complicated plan on which the national accounts are kept, is as absurd in principle as ridiculous in detail, with results unintelligible to the public and to accountants erroneous in figures and facts. It will be sufficient to give one instance in support of an otherwise incredible statement. The amount of Customs Revenue is to be got from two sources, viz., the Report published by the Commissioners of Customs, and the Statistical Abstract published by the Board of Trade. Surely these returns, being official, ought to give exactly the same result. What is the fact, however? Why, that for the year 1870, the former stated that the Customs Revenue was £23,182,276, while the latter gave the same item as £21,529,000, being a difference of £1,653,276 for that year; while the cost of collection for the same year according to the one was £799,351, and according to the other £979,918, being a difference of £180,567; making a total discrepancy for 1870 of £1,833,843, or more than the total payments of the Income Tax of Manchester, Liverpool, Birmingham, and London combined; or more than the whole assessment of Manchester. The other years are like unto 1870; and for the six years ending 1870, the difference between the two accounts is £7,936,105. Now, if these facts mean anything at all, they mean that we have such a miserably inefficient way of keeping the national accounts, that a mere huckster would be ashamed of it; or else during six years £7,936,105 sterling have vanished, and the taxpayers have a right to know where the money has gone. Nay, even in the balance-sheet for 1872, the Income is put down at £77,123,469, the Expenditure at £71,102,866, leaving a surplus of £6,020,573. Of the former, Mr. Morgan says: "The amount of Income is stated in the Cash Account, page 8, to be £76,608,770; but in page 12 the details of Income are stated to be £77,123,469; there is, consequently, a difference of £514,699 between the Cash Account and the Statement of Actual Income."

Now, having shown you how the stewards of the national purse fulfil their functions, and having hinted at the incapacity of the Government book-keepers, let us take the various items of expenditure which is indulged in by our Governments,—an annual expenditure consisting of nearly as many pounds as there are letters in the Bible.* The first item, on what is to the taxpayer the wrong side of the balance-sheet, is the item of £26,804,453 for the interest and management of the National Debt.

Mr. Disraeli has called the National Debt a "fleabite." I will not quarrel with that description. A

---

* The Expenditure for the year ending 31st March, 1871, was £71,102,896. The number of letters in the Bible is 71,329,600.

flea-bite may not be anything so serious as to render necessary the assistance of a doctor, but it is a very annoying, uncomfortable sort of thing. It is a thing which, like the toothache, no man can endure, and the sooner it is got rid of the better. Flea-bite as the debt is, it represents 5s. 4d. a minute, or £16 per hour, from the moment of Adam's creation; and did we not owe it, we could employ 15,384,615 men (above half the entire population of England, men, women, and children) for one year, at 20s. a-week. The history of this debt is one of the most disgraceful chapters in English history. It was nearly all contracted for foolish and wicked wars. Sir Robert Peel once said that it would have been better to have thrown the money into the sea. However, we have this debt, and the honour of the country demands that it shall be paid. We cannot repudiate our obligations; and all I can say with regard to it is, that it furnishes an additional reason why the upper classes should not be so squeamish about the working man paying his share of taxes. The National Debt was never contracted for the artizan. It was chiefly incurred when, more than now, the spending class was distinct from the paying class. It was invented at the same time as were Customs and Excise, and is a fit companion of the twin sisters. The debt was, comparatively speaking, trifling (a little over half a million) when William, of glorious memory landed on our shores in 1688. But William had a notion, peculiar to sovereigns, that it was necessary to maintain the "balance of power in Europe." I need hardly say that there is no such thing as the "balance of power." It is a mere figment proceeding from royal brains. That notion cost us about twelve millions. The advisers of Queen Anne pursued the same intermeddling policy, chiefly against France, which added twenty-four millions to the debt; while shortly afterwards the necessities of the Spanish war increased it still further. The war, and the subsidies, first for and then against the Pragmatic Sanction, added a few millions more; and then came the blind, reckless, mistaken rule of George III., which added seven hundred millions, the greater portion of the debt, and added it, too, for wars the most unjustifiable in history, and which can hardly now find a single advocate to defend them. They were the wars of aristocrats against the people. If I wished to produce historical evidence of this I should quote that passage from Sir Archibald Alison's history, in which he points out that, inasmuch as the passions of the people were aroused by the struggles for liberty which were taking place on the continent, and as there was a strong feeling in favour of innovation under the name of Reform growing up amongst the people at home, it was considered a wise policy to draw off the attention of the people from these things, and to arouse the ancient chivalry of the British people. We plunged therefore into a war with France, to put up the Bourbons, adding seven hundred millions to our debt. As my friend, Mr. J. Alun Jones, expresses it, "It was neither more nor less than a crusade against the growth of liberty abroad, and the progress of Reform at home." By an attempt to impose an indirect tax upon the Americans, striving, you see, to carry still further the principle that those who pay shall have no voice in the matter of spending, we not only lost our American colonies, but added eighty-two millions to the debt. Then we fought again against the French; this time to prevent them electing their own ruler, in the person of Napoleon I., and as to the stability of the success of that war, it may be remembered that, contrary to the obligations of the treaty which followed, we recognised his successor, Napoleon III., as soon as he succeeded in shedding sufficient blood to reach the throne. Gentlemen, I venture to assert that if the taxpayers had had a voice in the spending of their own money, this debt would never have been incurred. Balances of power,

Pragmatic Sanctions and dynastic wars may be a very nice thing for aristocrats and kings, but they are death to us. The people have to suffer for the faults of kings; and I do hope, therefore, that in any re-adjustment of taxation, the great landowners of this country will have the manliness to remember that the industrial classes have for generations paid the greatest portion of the interest on a debt which was not contracted either for them or by them.

I now come to the second item in the balance-sheet, viz., our defensive forces, which in 1873 cost us £24,956,200. We have the most expensive army and navy in the world, and as I have already pointed out by far the greater part of our expenditure is for war and war debt. As Leone Levi put it, "Between the legacy of past misdeeds and the excesses of recent exigencies, our military expenditure monopolises the best part of our public funds." The mind can hardly conceive what an enormous sum is spent upon soldiering and sailoring. Since the Crimean war, the Military and Naval expenditure has averaged more than £26,000,000 per annum. To aid the mind in comprehending this vast sum, a writer in the *Nonconformist* points out that according to the officially-published annual statistics, the total amount of coal produced in the United Kingdom has averaged for the past seven years an annual value of 22 million pounds sterling, or 4 millions less than the average cost of the army and navy. Hence all our coal mines united would not suffice to maintain our army and navy. And all the coal, iron, copper, lead, tin, zinc, silver and other metals produced in the United Kingdom have averaged in value (for seven years past) 37 million pounds per annum, or about 18 millions less than the year's expenditure for past and present wars. The total capital accumulated in the Post Office Savings' Bank was, in 1867, £9,749,929. The total capital in other Savings' Banks in the Kingdom in 1867, was £36,476,408. Total, £46,226,337. Hence the annual war expenditure (for present and past operations) far exceeds the total deposits of the industrial and economic classes invested in all the Savings' Banks. The total annual receipts of all the railways in the United Kingdom for passengers and goods are about 38 million pounds, or 17 millions less than the money demanded on account of war. The average value of all the wheat, barley, oats, maize, and flour imported into the United Kingdom (for seven years past) is 30 million pounds per annum, or only four millions more than the annual expenditure for army and navy alone, irrespective of national debt. The average value of the cotton imported into the United Kingdom (for seven years past) is 29 million pounds, exactly the cost of army and navy alone in 1868. No wonder the manufacturing population have to work hard to get a livelihood! All the paupers in the United Kingdom cost in the year 1870–71, £9,590,787, or about one-third of the expense of the army and navy.

Now, in criticising the expenditure for the army and the navy, I shall be at once told that having served in neither service I am not in a position to judge. But, gentlemen, when a man spends twice as much on an article as that article is worth, I say that he is extravagant, whether he purchase an Armstrong gun or a bale of cotton. Straws show which way the wind blows; and when I find the *Times* stating that five logs of wood — worth a few pounds — were towed in a special steamer from Sheerness to Chatham at a cost of £50; and that a bell was carried from Portsmouth to Liverpool at a cost of from £200 to £300, I have a notion that there is mismanagement at any rate in those departments, and I think it does not require a man to be either a soldier or sailor to see that. The

Admiralty recently made a peculiar bargain. They sold the *Medway* for £2,180, but promised to buy back the old stores out of her, which they actually did for £4,211. The Government, therefore, not only sold that ship for nothing, but they gave the purchaser £2,041 to take it away with him. This is not an exceptional thing; it is an instance under the mark. The practice is general, and sometimes the Government re-purchase the old stores at four or five times the price they get for the vessel. One vessel was sold for £300, and the copper re-purchased by the Government for £5,000, while the *Pelican* was sold by our authorities for £5,000, and the man who bought her sold her to the Portuguese Government for £40,000. I do not think it requires a man to be an admiral to see the folly of such transactions as these, and I can only say that there is in existence such evidence of gross neglect and mismanagement—if not worse—that it is appalling to think of it.

There might of course be some excuse if our army and navy were efficient. But such is not the case. You know that we now indulge occasionally in what are called Autumn Manœuvres. That is to say, we put a handful of men on the Downs, and play at fighting. Foreign military critics come over to watch us, and they go back laughing at our blundering. And well they might! For in a friendly country, with no real enemy to fight, we are unable to manage an army of the size of one Prussian army corps. The Commissariat continually breaks down, telegrams are sent to the wrong places for food, so that the men are sometimes twenty-four hours without rations, and the meat when it arrives is tainted. All this sort of thing is carried on at a great expense. Everything is dearly bought, and as a sample of how the money goes I will state that for the last Autumn Manœuvres horses were bought at £42 each, and were afterwards sold off at the rate of one hundred a week for £23 10s. each, the loss on this item alone being £35,000.

On the other hand, look at the cheap efficiency of the Prussian army. You know how a few years ago, on the shortest notice, the Prussian Government were able to put into the field a large army of 400,000 men, well equipped, well officered, and, as results proved, able to carry on a war with rapidity and success. Now, at the time Prussia was able to do all this so well, and we were able to do our little so badly, was the Prussian expenditure for defensive purposes so large as ours? On the authority of Mr. James White, the late member for Brighton, the whole revenue of Prussia, from all sources, for the year preceding the outbreak of the war, was two millions less than our expenditure for the year for army and navy alone. In fact, quite recently, Moltke has asked for a standing army of 401,000, which is only to cost £15,000,000, about the cost of our small army of less than 100,000 men; while France is proposing a standing army of no less than 1,200,000, which is only to cost about 25½ millions. "If an enemy landed on our coast," said Mr. Trevelyan in 1871, "we should be able to put 35,000 men in line; in other words, at twice the cost of the whole Prussian army, we should be able to bring into the field one Prussian corps."

I think I hear some one remind me of the difference in the military systems, inasmuch as there is conscription in the continental plan. I observe, *en passant*, that this forced service is a form of direct tax, and if it have no other recommendation, it must make the people take a great interest in the officering and cost of the army. But I do not forget this difference in the two systems. If the bulk of the expenditure for the army and navy were devoted to paying the men in the two services, the comparison would be fair; but such is not the fact; and if that be allowed for, we still compare very badly with other nations. No, gentlemen, it is not what we pay the rank and file, but maintaining crowds of useless and well-paid officers, that swells the estimates, and makes the cost of officering (*i.e.*, pay and allowances of officers) the British army no less than £20 13s. 4d. per man. Let me give you an instance. There are, you know, such beings as Honorary Colonels. These are men with very good salaries, and nothing to do. They usually hold their colonelcies in addition to something else, and are really for ornament, and nothing more. I remember that, at a public meeting in Kidderminster, a gentleman stated that he had served in a fighting regiment for seven years in India, and during the whole of that time he had never once seen his colonel. Upon hearing this, a man who had served in the Life Guards, which is not a fighting but a lounging regiment, said that his experience was quite different, as in his regiment there were swarms of colonels. So it is. We have swarms of these gentlemen paid from £900 to £2,000 a year each, and all the work they have to do is to receive their pay. The cost of these honorary colonels alone last year was £203,500; and when the Estimates were before the House last Session, Mr. G. O. Trevelyan moved that no further honorary colonels should be appointed. Of course, the motion was rejected. It was said that the honorary colonelcies were given as rewards of merit for distinguished services. I am afraid that if we investigate the careers of the fortunate holders of these sinecures, it will be found that they have done very little to merit such positions, beyond cringing to some relative in office, or serving some nobleman of position. Besides, if distinguished services are to be rewarded, let it be done openly and straightforwardly, and under the name of "reward," instead of by scattering broadcast appointments in which the duties are purely imaginary.

The great fact is, both the Army and the Navy are over-officered. Why do we require in this country three officers to do the work which is done in Prussia by two? In the Indian battalions in India, there are 1,500 superfluous claimants for pay, having pay and pensions amounting to the immense sum of £740,000 a year. Taking the English and Indian lists together, there are over 2,000 lieutenant-colonels and colonels, all of whom are supported by the State, though they have only a very small proportion of work to do. In the two branches of the Indian and English army, there are upwards of 800 generals, either active or idle. And all of these are in some shape or another a burden to the State. Of these 800 generals, how many are employed? There were employed, last year, 15 in administrative duties at home; 21 commanded at home, 12 in the colonies, and 43 in India — that is to say, 91 in all. Of these, 23 were colonels doing the work of brigadier-generals with local or temporary rank. Thus it will be seen that for every general who had the least atom of work to do, there were ten totally unemployed. The cause of this state of things, says Mr. Trevelyan, scandalous and cruel as it is to the taxpayers, is that successive governments have mixed up all their generals in one immense and undistinguishable list. Mr. Trevelyan also remarked that in a recent year the officers of the seven battalions of Guards had enjoyed among them just 23,648 days' leave, or at the rate of three months and a half for every officer.

It is hardly credible that we have nearly one admiral for each ship in the navy in commission, including block drill, gunnery, receiving, store, training and surveying ships; that we have three captains, or commanders, for every ship, big or little; and other officers are in proportion. Then in regard to the army, there is one general for every two regiments, and seventeen generals to spare. If we had ten more lieutenant-generals, there would be one for each regiment; in addition to which there is a major-general for each regiment, and 94 to spare. Of the colonels who have nothing to do, there are seven to each regiment, and 21 over; and of the lieutenant-colonels who are supposed to do the work which the colonels ought to do, there are nine to each regiment, and 125 over, and so on. When these facts are remembered, it will easily be seen how it is we have such an enormous expenditure for naval and military purposes. If there be one place more than another where more work and less play are required, it is in those departments which provide us with "an army of regiments that cannot march, and a fleet of ships that cannot swim."

It is not only amongst the officers that the recklessly extravagant way of doing business displays itself. It permeates the whole system. In almost every thing that is done, from building an iron-clad to buying an anchor, from appointing the "First Lord" to promoting a cadet, the efficiency of the service suffers in some way or other. When Mr. W. E. Baxter took office, he found that bribery, corruption and fraud were so great in the Admiralty Department that no respectable firm would do business with it; and although an example was made by exposing two officials, yet the whole system is so laced round with trickery that the conviction and its results, however just as a punishment, proved of no avail as a deterrent. It has never yet been satisfactorily explained how one favoured firm has been paid thousands upon thousands above the market price for anchors, and anchors, too, which have long been disused by the Merchant Service, as being far too dear and too inefficient when compared with the one which is used on the Queen's yacht alone of all the ships paid for by taxes; and to other firms thousands upon thousands in excess of the real price of cables. It is not generally known that when the market price for oil was £126 a ton the Admiralty paid £134. It would have been more satisfactory, too, if the vast quantity of pig iron which paves Devonport Dockyard had been either used for its proper purpose or sold. Neither is it pleasant to hear that Deptford Dockyard had been sold privately to a friend of the chief solicitor in the Naval Department; and that the sale was not completed for twelve months, during which the purchaser transferred his interest to the Corporation of London, and by that transfer, without the payment of a single penny, he put into his pocket £21,000, which ought to have gone into the National Exchequer. Now, £21,000 is about the same amount as the City of Bath paid in income tax in 1870, the year the transaction took place, so that the good people of that city, who have been so prominent in their outcry against the principle of the tax, have the additional chagrin of knowing that not only have they had to pay a tax which was unjustly levied, but that having paid it, the whole amount went into the pocket of one favoured individual for no earthly reason whatever.

When men in high positions are guilty of such things, we must not be surprised to find that the subordinates take upon themselves to copy the example of their superiors. Thus we have the farce known as a " Dockyard Sale." No intending purchaser is admitted to the sale until he has first paid £5 for a catalogue, the amount to be returned if he make a purchase. The practical result of this is, that a certain number of fellows form a "ring," to take an American word, and arrange the sale, and after the sale is over they adjourn to a neighbouring public-house and divide their profits, the whole process having the euphonious title of a "knock-out." Thus it is that overcoats, lined with wool all through, and almost new, go for six shillings each; and Highland beavers, with ostrich plumes, of which the first-cost was £3 19s. each, for 3s. 6d.

It must not be supposed either that these sales are of surplus stores. If one department wanted certain things, and another department had too many of them, the most natural process would be to take from that department which hath, and transfer it to that which hath not. That, however, is too direct a way for departments to go. Their plan is to sell off at a great loss in the way above described, and to purchase new stores for the other department; and the new stores purchased for one department are very often the very same as those which have previously been sold as "old stores" by another. It is not therefore surprising to hear that, recently, twelve tons of soldiers' buttons were sold by the Government as "old metal," although the packages had never been opened, much less used, and, if rumour be correct, they were resold to the Government as new buttons. The *West Country Lantern* is a Plymouth newspaper, which, being published near Devonport Dockyard, has wisely kept its eyes open on the doings of the pig-iron paved yard. I hope it will continue to expose all the abuses it can find out. The other day this newspaper drew attention to what it calls "one of those extraordinary phenomena, a dockyard sale." "We see," said the editor "among the articles to be sold are nineteen boilers, seven lathes, by Glasgow makers, fourteen anchors, two steam engines, eighty-five tons of iron, *six tons of nails*, fifteen tons of galvanized wire, and lots of other useful articles, and also lots of worn-out things and rubbish. Last year heaps of things were sold that had not been used, and are continually wanted—things new and unused—perhaps slightly tarnished by lying by. Brass and copper, tools, instruments, fittings, stores, etc., were sold by the ton (*new, good, and unused*), that would have to be immediately *replaced*; and it has been repeatedly stated that in the *same week many things were rebought from the purchasers at from twice to thrice the cost at which they were sold*—there not being sufficient left in store for the daily wants of the yard. Now, why should they sell the iron or the nails, which are both articles of daily need? Last year, a broker bought some cwts. of brass screws quite a bargain; why were they sold? They are constantly required in ship-building. If there happens to be a surplus of stock, the reasonable plan is to suspend the purchase of fresh stock for a time, and not to sell off the surplus at what it will fetch, as might be justifiable for a tradesman in difficulties. Last year heaps of unused brass and copper articles were sold, which would have to be replaced at double the cost which they fetched at the Dockyard sale, and some taxpayers present were puzzled to account for such folly, and indignant also.

They thought it might have something to do with the making accounts look pleasant at a certain time; but if such is the case, 'tis greater folly than that committed by the silly management of a mismanaged railway in paying swinging dividends out of the spare capital. Bearing on this is the fact repeated to us by several naval officers of a ship returning to port, of *unused boatswains' and engineers' stores, instruments, tools, being thrown overboard to make things come square with the accounts at home,* so much being allowed for use, and therefore so much *must* be used up, and if not used properly, must be otherwise made away with; hence this reckless folly and waste. Why, twenty millions won't do for our navy a few years hence with such wasteful and incompetent management."

One more instance: The treatment of two ships at Portsmouth affords a striking sample of the way in which Her Majesty's Navy is managed by the Board of Admiralty and its functionaries. The *Prince Regent*, built in 1823, as a three decked sailing ship to carry 120 guns, and afterwards " converted " into a two decked screw liner, was recently broken up by order of "my Lords." Her framework and timbers generally were so sound that she would have been good for some years' further service. Another ship, the *Boscawen*, built in 1844, as a sailing two-decker, and of late employed as a training ship for boys at Portland, having been sent to Portsmouth for a thorough overhaul, was found to be so unsound that the truest economy would obviously have been to break her up. But not so thought the Board; for the sound ship was broken up, and the rotten one was ordered to be repaired!

One word more, and I will leave this branch of the subject. I wish to impress upon you that all this has taken place not ages upon ages ago, but in the present day, and is now going on. I wish I could hold out any hope that the House of Commons would soon improve in this respect. "My experience," once said Mr. Bernal Osborne, "has taught me that the Members of Parliament are the worst body of men that can be found to control the expenditure of the nation;" and when you find the House so careless, you can hardly blame the Departments. Only last Session it was determined to continue the fortification of Alderney. The *Sailing Directions for the Channel* would serve to convince any one not too stupid and self-willed for conviction, that there is not, and never was, any occasion for spending a penny on the fortification of Alderney, although a sum approaching to £2,000,000 of the public money has been thus utterly thrown away. Alderney is a place to which all captains give the widest berth they can, and never come near if they can possibly avoid it. Alderney Race is never safe excepting in the very calmest weather. No large vessel can get near the island, as it is surrounded on all sides by dangerous rocks, the enumeration and description of which occupy full five pages of the *Sailing Directions.* The only two spots where a landing can be effected have been converted into harbours of refuge, which are only available for vessels whose hard fate drives them near the spot, at high water, and when the wind is not from the east. But for risk to the vessel, officers, and crew, it would be well to sentence Lord Viscount Halifax, and my Lords of the Admiralty, and all who have taken part in this further most needless waste of the public money, to a cruise in the Warrior round the island, with obligation to land every day, for a month, or until they were fully convinced that the fortification of Alderney, either to " watch Cherbourg," or for any other purpose, is one of the most stupendous follies that ever entered the mind of man. Rather than these extravagances should be sanctioned, I would much prefer to see done what has been done before, and for anything I know may be done now, viz., that the Lords of the Admiralty send a gunboat down to the Frith of Forth to take care of the Duke of Buccleugh's fisheries, as was done in 1869, and another to be similarly employed on behalf of the Herne Bay Oyster Company.

Well, I now pass on to the £19,341,843 spent last year on the Civil Service, which has been described as that fund from which members of Parliament are paid for sitting behind the Government, never saying anything, but always voting as they are told. Of course some excuse has to be made for finding opportunities for supporters and their friends. This is generally done by what is called the " Reorganisation of Office," which means neither more nor less than pensioning off a lot of men in the enjoyment of good salaries, and appointing others in their places; or else pensioning off clerks in one department, and appointing fresh ones in another. The Government no more think of transferring clerks from an over-stocked to an under-stocked office, than they would think of transferring stores from one dockyard to another, and if they attempt it they blunder so that the attempt is a failure. It has often been pointed out that a great saving might be effected, if, instead of pensioning off redundant clerks in one department and appointing others to departments which are short-handed, the overplus clerks in the crowded office were transferred to those departments which required them. A man may be very unfit for the department to which he was first appointed, but very well fitted for other departments. He may be useless in the War Office, but a very jewel in the Census Office, and yet it seldom suggests itself to the official mind to remove him whence he is useless to the place where he might be useful. Recently an attempt has been made to do this, and the bungling which accompanied the attempt, consequent upon red-tape and departmental jealousy, is quite worthy of our Governments.

It appears that on the 21st February, 1872, the Exchequer and Audit Department wrote to the Treasury stating that the existing staff was insufficient for the work of the office, and asking for sixteen additional "examiners," which, it was suggested, might be supplied from the "Redundant List." This letter lay idle at the Treasury Office until the 13th April (twenty days), when a letter was written to the War Office, and another to the Admiralty, asking them each to find eight clerks to fill up the sixteen vacancies. The Admiralty took forty-three days to consider this letter, and the War Office eighty-two, when the former stated

(16th May) that they had clerks willing to accept the transfer on condition that their "standing" dated from the time they entered the service of the Government as temporary and not as permanent clerks (which, of course, affected their length of service, and consequently their salary and pension); while the latter (on the 24th June) stated that they could not find any clerks willing to be transferred, being unwilling, it is to be presumed, to relinquish the honour attached to the War Office clerks of being the best waltz dancers in the west end of London. In the meantime (6th June) the Exchequer and Audit Department had again written to the Treasury complaining of the delay in answering their letter of the 21st February, stating that "unless the assistance be speedily afforded, it would be impossible for the department to report satisfactorily upon the accounts within the time prescribed by Parliament." Consequently, on the 8th of June, the Treasury wrote to the Admiralty agreeing with the request of the clerks that their "standing" should date from the time of their entering Her Majesty's service as temporary clerks; and on the 11th of the same month the Admiralty furnished a list of eight redundant clerks. In consequence of the refusal of the clerks in the War Office, the Treasury wrote on the 29th June to the

K

Customs Department, making a similar request for four redundant clerks, which was not answered until the 15th July (17 days), during which time one of the Admiralty clerks had declined the offer of transfer and found another in his place. These lists were duly sent to the Exchequer and Audit Department, upon which that department took offence, that the nominations had been made without consulting the "Head of the Department," as stipulated in the first letter of the correspondence (21st February). To this the Treasury snappishly replied that they had the power, under the 8th section of the Exchequer and Audit Act, to nominate without consulting the Comptroller and Auditor General, but that they had no objections to obtain certificates of the proficiency of the nominated clerks from the Civil Service Commissioners. These, however, the Civil Service Commissioners refused to grant unless the Comptroller of the Exchequer and Audit approved of the nominations, which the latter refused to do unless the clerks were subjected to additional examination. The Treasury, not to be baffled, then said they should transfer the clerks without such certificates, repeating their power under the Exchequer and Audit Act, and accordingly, on the 6th February, 1873 (a few days within twelve months after the original application), the Treasury told five of the clerks they must go and take their places in the Exchequer and Audit Department on a six months' probation. The Comptroller of the Exchequer and Audit Department thereupon said that when the first month's salary of the newly transferred clerks became due, he should decline to pay them, as he would not take upon himself the responsibility of putting into the estimates the expenses of so irregular a proceeding; and so the matter has rested there since the 19th of March, 1873. This is only a meagre outline of the correspondence, and can give but a vague idea of the red-tape employed in this simple little question which any man of common sense could have settled in ten hours, but which is not settled yet. Orders in Council, Treasury minutes, and Acts of Parliament and other documents were quoted wholesale, until at last the muddle was so great that the best way to bring about the crisis was for the Audit Department to refuse to pay the newly transferred clerks, and wait for the result, which I do as anxiously as the Comptroller of the Exchequer and Audit Department.

The return from which I have got this information consists of fifty-two pages of printed matter, and contains the correspondence between twenty-four officials, besides numerous other documents; and all on account of the transference from one department to another of a few clerks, the highest salaried amongst them being £150 a-year, which transfer is not accomplished yet. Another question naturally suggests itself, viz.: How *dare* the redundant War Office clerks refuse to be transferred? Why was not the option given them —. transference or dismissal? And, indeed, taking all things into consideration, it just shows the circumlocution, the red-tape, and the how-not-to-do-it, which are the guiding stars of departmental management. It will readily be admitted that under such a system of bungling and blundering, sinecures may be created *ad infinitum.* Useless offices breed like maggots and flies, by corruption—and are like maggots and flies ever breeding it.

Leone Levi says: "It is the expenditure which determines the income, and not the income the expenditure." In this, Mr. Leone Levi is decidedly wrong. That is how it should be; but so elastic are the resources that Governments feel they have the power to spend the largest amount they can get voted. "The House of Commons," once said Mr. John Bright, "does nothing to check extravagance; it encourages it. Its members are not so much of the tax-paying as the tax-consuming class. They come from, and they chiefly represent, those whose families have for generations considered the taxation of the people as their lawful patrimony." Every experienced member in the House knows that the extravagance in certain Government departments increases just in proportion to the amount of money they can obtain from the Treasury. Now, one of the simplest ways of spending money is to pay a lot of men large salaries for doing nothing; and this system is so well acknowledged by the upper classes, that cases are known in which an annuity has been left to a younger son, to be paid "until such time as he receives a Government appointment," and the whole method has been aptly described as "a sytem of out-door relief for the younger sons of the aristocracy."

Not long ago, Mr. Lowe stated that he knew of a case of a man getting £500 a year, who was only fit to, and did only, tie up and address parcels, not being competent to do anything else; and even when Chancellor of the Exchequer, the same gentleman said he was unable to say whether that state of things had ceased. Mr. Walmsley, the late Clerk of the Parliament, who retired last year on his full salary of £1,150 a year, received his appointment before he was fourteen years old; and I might spend hour after hour in the bare enumeration of the jobs exhibited in the sinecure offices. A paragraph was recently published which must have astonished all who read it. It appeared in a periodical usually well-informed on political matters, viz., *Vanity Fair,* and was as follows:—" There are things done at the War Office, the Colonial Office, the Custom House, and the Foreign Office, enough to make the hair of sober folk to stand upon end. Not long ago I was dining with a Cabinet Minister, when his private secretary laughingly pointed out that an individual clerk in a public department had actually paid £28,000 of public money in one year under a snug family arrangement to his brother-in-law; and that the same gentleman—whose very name is unknown beyond Downing-street, but which is quite at Mr. Vernon Harcourt's service—was in the habit of distributing royal rewards and sinecures to his friends, which rewards varied from £1,000 to £4,000 a year. He had the power of giving a man lieutenant-general's rank, too, though he never served a day in the army or out of it; and by these means he drove such a thriving trade that his business profits out of public money considerably exceeded £30,000 a year."

I have endeavoured to discover the leech who is

thus allowed to suck at the public purse; and although I have not succeeded in ascertaining his name, I have received ample information to lead me to believe that the above-quoted paragraph states a fact; and if the person suspected of being the individual referred to be actually the man, he has also been honoured with a peerage, though I should have thought that the quiet, easy, gentle way in which he has taken the widows' mites, and the hard-earned wages of poor and ignorant agricultural labourers, and builded for himself therefrom a fortune, which is the price of blood if anything ever was in this world, ought to have been honoured in quite a different way.

It was Dan O'Connell, I think, who used to tell an anecdote showing that the "Elliot" family had such influence that anyone bearing that name could easily obtain a Government appointment. There was much of truth in the notion, because hundreds and hundreds of appointments are now made for no other reason than that the appointees are relatives of the governing families. It cannot fail to be noticed how comfortably family arrangements are made, and that Allen, Anderson, Baker, Elliot, Hamilton, and a score of others seem to be favoured households. The following list of the pickings of the Romilly family is given as a fair sample of this kind of nepotism:—Lord Romilly (late Master of the Rolls), official salary, £6,000; Edward Romilly, Esq. (Audit Office), £2,000; Charles Romilly, Esq. (Crown Office), £1,200; Col. F. Romilly (Customs' Commissioner), £1,000; Hon. Edward Romilly (Secretary to Lord Justice), £500; Hon. John Romilly (Clerk of Records), £1,200; Hon. William Romilly (Clerk in Enrolment Office), £1,200. All these drew their salaries at one time, and with the exception of the first named (who has a pension) are drawing them still.

It is not surprising that with such a system scattering sinecures broadcast among our aristocratic families, there should be an equally scandalous system of granting pensions. Pensions are bad things in themselves; they are a premium on improvidence. By all means, pay a man a fair day's wage for a fair day's work, but let him know that he must, by prudence and care, prepare for a rainy day. The taxpayers receive no pensions, and "in no case," says Montesquieu, "ought the people to be deprived of the means to meet their real wants in order to provide for the imaginary wants of the State." Of course, there are seeming exceptions. When a man has performed some great service to his country, he deserves a reward, and if he have perished in his work it would be ungrateful indeed on the part of the State to allow his family to suffer any loss or privation, while of course a person who is induced to give up a lucrative profession for a public office, which he loses with a change of Ministry, requires more than the annual salary of his office after he has ceased to hold it. There is, however, no reason why a pension should be given year after year and generation after generation for ever. Because the Duke of Schomberg was killed at the Battle of the Boyne in 1690, by an accidental shot from his own side, we are now paying his descendant £2,160 a year, and will continue to do so until a loud expression on the part of the public against such a thing demands its cessation. The Duke of Marlborough was certainly a brilliant soldier in the days of Queen Anne, but surely he was amply recompensed at the time, while the succeeding Dukes have each received £4,000 a year. The present Duke receives it, and his successors will continue to do so. That is a pension that may be very well done away with. For sixty years we have paid £2,000 a year for the military services rendered to this country in 1814 by Lord Combermere and his descendants, and a similar sum for a similar time to Lord Exmouth (for naval services) and his descendants, and these ought to be done away with on the deaths of the present recipients. Who Mrs. Sarah Hamilton was, and who her children may be, and what either one or the other has done for the State, I know not; but for the last seventy-six years the sum of £47,502 10s. 8d. has gone to them in the shape of pensions, while nine more of the "Hamiltons" are also in receipt of annual incomes for doing nothing. We have the largest pension list in the world, and by the process of "reorganising the department" mentioned before, it is increasing every year. The Estimates for 1873-4 include a reinforcement of 187 recruits to this list. Of these, 96 owe their release from work, or rather from office, to ill-health and infirmity, 38 to reduction, revision, reorganisation or abolition of office, 34 to age, and 19 to causes not specified.

With regard to those gentlemen who have retired from office on account of ill-health and old age, I am afraid that in a great number of the cases the reason stated is a mere excuse. Bismarck says that those widows of soldiers who receive pensions live a long time; and anyone who looks over the pension list of England will find that the death-rate of those pensioners who are ill is much lower than the death-rate of non-pensioned persons who are well. I find that Mr. R. R. Mudge, of the Woods and Works Office, retired on account of ill-health in 1843, and he is still drawing his pension, having been ill for no less a period than thirty-one years. Mr. Matthew Carter has suffered from a still longer illness, having retired on account of ill-health thirty-four years ago, since which time he has regularly drawn his pension; while Mr. R. B. Hoppner, formerly a consul at Venice, was taken ill in 1825, and remained in that deplorable condition for forty-seven years. A very peculiar case is that of Sir Alexander Y. Spearman, who was formerly in the Treasury, from which he retired on account of ill-health upon a pension of £1,350. He had not been ill long when he was appointed Comptroller of the National Debt Office, at a salary of £1,500 a year, in consideration of which the pension from his former office was reduced to £1,000 a year. After Sir Alexander Spearman had received £1,000 a year for being too ill to work in one department, and £1,500 a year for at the same time controlling another department for about thirty years, he last year retired on a further pension of his full salary, £1,500 a year. The last I heard of Sir Alexander Y. Spearman was that he had fallen ill again. Probably, therefore, he is to receive another appointment; and indeed it would be an interesting experiment for a Government to try how many pensions and how many sinecures can possibly be piled on the shoulders of one man. Hitherto such experiments have been eminently successful, as the case of the Rev. Thomas Thurlow abundantly proves. This fortunate clergyman, a nephew of Lord Chancellor Thurlow—or "thorough low" as he was nicknamed—was appointed at an early age to the office of Prothonotary of the Court of Durham, to the see of which his father had been appointed by the same dispenser of good gifts. The nephew was also made a Hanaper* Keeper; and a third office, that of Patentee of Bankrupts, was also given him. The reverend gentleman has at this day a compensation allowance for all these offices. The amount of that compensation is now £11,779 5s. 5d. per annum, and the veteran preacher of the Gospel has drawn most of it for upwards of forty years. This lucky Christian had other offices which are now abolished; but taking those from which he still derives an income, he has already received £402,788 13s. of the public money for which he has done no work whatever, beyond signing a receipt for the money which has been given him.

* Waste paper basket.

The Pension List ought to be reduced at once by at least one million; and the whole system ought to be gradually abolished. It is foolish to speak of vested interests. We are not bound by what was done in Queen Anne's reign, or in that of George II.; and as some pensions and sinecures have been abolished, or commuted, or altered in some way or other, there are precedents for the reform I am advocating. We are not called upon to support Royal bastards to the fifth and sixth generation, nor to pay pensions for we know not what. Let a searching enquiry be made into the folly of continuing these parasitical growths which are gradually spreading themselves more and more over the departments of the State. Perhaps, if enquiries were made, some of the recipients of these pensions would be so conscience-stricken that they would refuse them. Such a thing has been known. Some time ago it was decided that certain ladies receiving pensions should state the grounds of their claim. Several of them declined to do so, thus preferring to lose their pensions, rather than put in writing the true position they held. There is a limit even to the impudence of shameless claimants. I say that in reducing these pensions the pruning knife should not be spared. The exact amount of them it is difficult to ascertain in the present jumbled state of the national accounts; and I am quite sure it is beyond the ability of the blundering Audit Office to find out what we waste in this respect. Mr. Lowe puts it down at about £5,000,000 a year; and Mr. Rylands has pointed out that the pensions to the persons who have been in the Civil Service alone are more than the rental of the great town of Birmingham. Let the people of Ipswich remember that it takes more than they pay in income-tax to pay the pensions of the Rev. Thomas Thurlow alone. Ipswich has representatives in Parliament; let them see to it. Nearly the whole of the amount paid in income-tax by the city of Hereford is required for the hereditary pension to the Duke of Marlborough. Hereford is well represented in the House; let its members see to it. And so on with other places. If a lot of the moderate sized towns, like Kendal, Buckingham, Bedford, Dorchester, and a great many others which return members to Parliament, would only remember that the whole of the amount paid by them respectively in income-tax goes to support a pensioner, and if they would then impress the great fact upon their representatives in the House of Commons, the system I have spoken of, and which I characterise as venal, corrupt, dishonest, cruel, and disgraceful, would not last very long.

This is not the place to weary you with long and tedious accounts of the incapacity of almost each department to do its business. I must refer you to the various Blue Books on the subject which have been published, all of which show that a system of reckless extravagance prevails in every kind of transaction, from those of the greatest amount to those of the least. It may be surprising to some persons to learn that when they go to law they pay for it in taxes, as well as by fees, and that when they do not go to law they pay a share of the expenses of those who do, however private may be the quarrel. I am not speaking of the Criminal Courts. Of course, we must all contribute to the cost of the means taken for the prevention of crime. I am speaking of those Courts in which private squabbles are settled. Why should the public pay the expenses of a woman obtaining a divorce from her husband, or of a man recovering a debt, or of the litigation which follows a carelessly worded contract? I am aware that some people have such a strong affection for the feudal system—under which every freeman, if not a judge, was at any rate obliged to go bail for his neighbours—that they hold that we are all interested in and protected by the decisions of the Courts of Law, and ought therefore to pay our share of the expenses of these Courts.

I maintain, however, that we are only interested to the same extent that we are interested in the health of our citizens, and while, doubtless, all ought to bear the burdens of the suppression of violence and crime, and the prevention of epidemics, yet only the parties concerned are interested in the recovery from sickness, or the interpretation of a deed. We ought no more to pay a portion of the expenses of A for the recovery of his debt from B, than we ought to contribute to the fees of Dr. C. for the cure he has effected on D. We are, however, taxed heavily for law. That is to say, our Courts of Law are not self-supporting. Thus the deficiency in the Common Law Courts in 1871–72 was £86,000, which includes £13,000 on account of sinecure offices abolished in 1838, and another large item is on account of pensions. These figures are *exclusive* of the salaries and pensions of the judges and masters. So with regard to the other Courts. The Courts of Bankruptcy cost the country £75,000 a year; the County Courts, £195,000; the Court of Probate and Divorce £60,000, and so on through all the Courts, the climax being reached at the Land Registry Court, the expenses of which are ten times its fees, though it is very clear that those who derive advantage from the existence of the Court ought to pay for it, not the masses of taxpayers who have not an inch of land to claim, hold, or defend. All this is exclusive of judges' salaries, pensions, etc., and the loss upon the courts in Scotland and Ireland. A Committee of the House of Commons has decided that an expenditure of £1,750,000 in connection with the Law Courts requires "a searching investigation;" and I have it on good authority that a loss of £1,351,000 a year might be avoided. Now this is more than Manchester, Salford, Birmingham, London (city), Bury, Rochdale, Stockport, Ashton-under-Lyne, Oldham, Wigan, and Warrington combined pay in income-tax; and I must confess that I think it an unfair thing that taxes to such an enormous amount should be levied, not for the prevention of crime, or for the protection of the person, but for the settlement of what are to all intents and purposes private disputes. This is the more apparent when it is remembered that while the cost of the Admiralty Court in London is between twice and three times its receipts, that in Liverpool is self-supporting.

When I find that the British taxpayer paid £68 for the conveyance of Prince Christian from Dover to Calais — and I only take this as a case representing a great many similar ones —; that we were nearly saddled with an additional £11,000 on account of the Zanzibar "job"; that a subordinate at South Kensington Museum can steal £8,000 before he is found out, and still more recently a clerk in a police office several thousands before he is discovered; that to a great extent compensations, superannuations, etc., follow no fixed rule, and are not regulated by statute, but depend on the whim of an individual; that judges have the power of making appointments and fixing salaries, without end, as far as I can gather from official reports; that some Courts cost three times their receipts, and yet no attempt has been made to revise them; that there are two judges where one would be sufficient; and a whole host of other things which mean jobbery, extravagance, and iniquity; I am not surprised that a Committee of the House of Commons recommends that a "searching investigation" should be made, and clothes its recommendation in such terms that it means "jobbery" is the order of the day. I agree, also, that it should be seen "whether and in what manner the large number of persons formerly connected with Courts of Justice, who are in receipt of compensation on abolition of office, might be utilised by being appointed to other offices in these establishments." But, above all things, I am glad to see that so strongly is the Committee referred to impressed with the iniquitous state of affairs at present that, with true and manly courage, it has recommended that, pending legislation, "no vacancy in a salaried office in any of these establishments be permanently filled up, *without the previous consent in writing of the First Lord of the Treasury;*" and "that every person so appointed should take office subject to such alterations as to its duties, salaries and pensions (whether on superannuation or abolition) as may be determined by Parliament." In the former part of this address I pointed out what were the duties of the Government "Whip." Let me tell you that his title is an appropriate one. It is "Patronage Secretary to the Treasury," for which he gets a salary of £2,000. It is a disgraceful thing that our Governments have to indulge in what is nothing else than wholesale bribery; but it is infinitely more disgraceful that £2,000 a year should be taken from the people's exchequer to pay for services which, to say the least of them, are of a doubtful character.

If further evidence of the state of our Departments be required, there are the utterances of Mr. W. E. Baxter, who, when in office, made praiseworthy attempts to conduct the work of the State in a business-like and common-sense fashion. One of the greatest evils imaginable is, "voting money on account" before the estimates are presented. You may be sure that it is all spent, and the estimates are framed accordingly. The money is spent first, and then asked for afterwards. Mr. Baxter himself, when a member of the Government, has been obliged to confess in the House of Commons that such was the case.

It appears that "the Treasury claims the right to judge every measure increasing or tending to increase" the civil expenditure. The Treasury, however, does not seem to care much about this power of supervision, and seldom uses it, except when there is an application made for additional clerks or advanced salaries; so that a whole office may be idle — as is indeed the case with the Board of Trade — because the Treasury is too lazy or too unwilling to review the Departments. I repeat that it must not be forgotten, however, as Mr. Baxter stated in his evidence, that when a Government is weak, or is about to retire, it has its hands to strengthen, and its friends to reward. The Government then soon finds out that departments want revising, and the result is that a large number of additional appointments are made. This is mildly expressed by the Committee, whose report I have often quoted, as follows: — "When legislation affects the business of a particular department, the occasion is sometimes taken to revise its strength; and inquiries of this kind are also from time to time instituted at the suggestion of the *political* heads of the Treasury."

I ask any sensible man, Can the departments of the State be in an efficient condition when such things are practised? Again, look at the Scudamore affair. Mr. Scudamore, you may remember, is the officer of the Post Office who intercepted and delayed telegrams sent from one person to another,— a transaction which has never been equalled since the opening of letters by Sir James Graham. He was justly censured for this; but we had scarcely got over our surprise at his conduct, when we were startled by the announcement that he had misappropriated the Savings Banks' deposits. The Post Office Scandal, as it has been called, briefly comes to this. Mr. Scudamore, a clerk in the Post Office Department, applied Post Office revenues and Savings Banks' deposits to purposes useful and necessary, no doubt, but for which Parliamentary provision ought to have been made. This had been going on for three or four years, to such an extent that a sum of £800,000 had been thus misappropriated. This was done without let or hindrance from Postmaster General, Audit Board, Lords of the Treasury, or National Debt Commissioners, whose duty it was to see to the proper investment of the Savings Banks' deposits. Of course, Mr. Scudamore received no personal benefit from this loose method of doing business, as the money was devoted to the public service. But, supposing that some one with the same power had been dishonest, and instead of devoting the Savings Banks', deposits to the public good, had taken them himself, and lived in splendid retirement in some luxurious country with which we have an imperfect extradition treaty, he could have done so as easily as Mr. Scudamore exceeded his duty. All this in spite of an Audit Office, consisting of a Comptroller, at £2,000 a-year; an Assistant-Comptroller, at £1,000 a-year; a Secretary, and a large staff, the whole costing £42,000 a-year; the special business of the department being to see that the other departments keep within their tether, and that the special sums voted by Parliament shall be appropriated to the purposes for which they were voted. I am speaking on good authority when I say that there are several officers in the various departments of the Civil Service, who, if they want money for a few days, can draw a cheque for any reasonable sum they please. Indeed, the words of Mr. Gladstone, when applied to the departments, some years ago, apply with only slightly diminished force to the state of things now. "Vaccillation," he said, "uncertainty, costliness, extravagance, meanness, and all the vices that can be enumerated are united in our present system. The money of the country is wasted; and, I believe, such are the evils of the system, that nothing short of a revolutionary reform will ever bring them to an end."

There are other considerations besides the mere one of economy, important as that is. "The Services" are discontented. This is very natural. Those who work hard for little pay, are naturally displeased at seeing lisping, foppish sinecurists loitering about the offices on big salaries. When an unfair appointment is made, it naturally offends those who have been thereby, as it were, thrust out of their turn. When a gentleman is put into an office, because he has an uncle or a cousin in the Cabinet, and for no other reason, it is not highly satisfactory to those who have been toiling and moiling — in the way that many in the Civil Service do toil and moil — for several years, in the hope of getting that appointment; when appointments are made, not because they are wanted, but to please Lord Privyseal, or to fulfil the promises of the Government Whip, there is the usual grumble, "no chance of promotion in an overstocked department."

Of course, things mended a little when the Civil Service Examinations were instituted, but even yet influence can get over these; and recently a candidate who was "plucked" received an appointment over the heads of those who had been years in office, and who, of course, looked upon it as a piece of favouritism. Indeed, I cannot better illustrate the discontent which prevails in the Civil Service than by stating that they issue an ably-conducted weekly magazine of sixteen pages, at threepence each number, called the *Civilian*, which has now passed its two hundred and fiftieth number, and is in its seventh volume, and nearly the whole of its pages are filled with one wail of complaint and lamentation against the way in which the Civil departments of the State are conducted. Here, then, is the testimony of the Civil servants themselves, and I am sure it will be acknowledged that a minimum of work only can be got out of men in a state of chronic discontent.

There is a still higher question. I will not complain—though in my heart I do—of rich and powerful Ministers of State receiving large pensions for life when they have only been a short time in office; but I do feel ashamed that men, rich and powerful men, whom the people call, and probably think, "right honourable," should declare that it is their "poverty and not their will consents." It is not generally known, that by an Act passed in the reign of William IV., an ex-minister, to receive his pension, must declare that without it he is unable to maintain his position. How many noblemen and "right honourables," now alive, have made that declaration, knowing it to be entirely false! Even the Government itself violates the spirit if not the letter of the law, by interfering (through clubs, of course,) with the elections;* sometimes foolishly, as in a case I know of, when the Reform Club man went to the Tory agent, by mistake, to bring out a Liberal whom the Government wanted in the House. The plucky little borough, however, wouldn't stand it, and, rejecting the Government Liberal, sent one of its own. When in these high quarters the things I have mentioned take place day after day, and you find them prevailing through chief clerks, second clerks, messengers, and, I dare say,

* In 1779, the House of Commons resolved:—" That it is highly criminal for any minister or ministers, *or any other servant* of the crown of Great Britain, directly or indirectly, to make use of the power of his office, in order to influence the election of members of Parliament, and that an attempt to exercise that influence is an attack upon the dignity, the honour, and the independence of Parliament, an infringement of the rights and the liberties of the people, and an attempt to sap the basis of our free and happy constitution."

down to the very office cleaners; and when you remember also that the Army and Navy are tarred with the same brush, you will easily see that from the top to the bottom nearly every one has his eye open to his own interests at the cost of the taxpayers. It is the Five Alls over again. "I rule all," said the king; "I pray for all," said the parson; "I plead for all," said the lawyer; "I fight for all," said the soldier; and "I pay for all," said the labourer. How much lower this tainting influence will go, I don't know; but it has already reached the recruiting sergeant. Supposing a sergeant enlists a man,— a half-intoxicated man,—the chances are that in a few hours the man will repent and wish himself free again. The sergeant tells him that if he can raise what is called the "smart-money," say twenty-one shillings, before the day after to-morrow, he can be freed. The man does so, and hands it to the sergeant. Now, notice. If no one knows of the transaction, and the sergeant generally takes care that nobody does, he pockets the guinea. If the man cannot raise the money, the sergeant still gets something for enlisting him; and if the poor fellow raises the "smart-money," and others do know of it, the sergeant gets a share of it. So that any way the sergeant "stands to win," as the betting men say. To what extent this practice exists I don't know, but that it does exist I know very well. You cannot blame the sergeant very much. It is in the nature of man to copy his betters; and, after all, it is only carrying out the policy which is winked at, if not initiated, at head quarters.

Well, gentlemen, there is one more item on which I will touch. Besides the numerous sinecure appointments held by the members of the Royal Family, we give the Princess Royal £8,000 a-year; the Prince of Wales £40,000 a-year; the Princess of Wales £10,000 a-year; Prince Alfred £15,000 a-year;* Prince Arthur £15,000 a-year; the Princesses Alice, Helena, and Louise £6,000 a-year each; and handsome sums to other princes and princesses of the blood-royal. In addition to these, we give to Her Majesty an annual sum of £385,000 a-year. Now, I am saying nothing against all this. If the people of this country like such expensive things as an Army and Navy and a Royal Family, they must pay for them; but I do object to the absurd and unbecoming way in which the Queen is obliged—I say obliged, because she has no control over it—to spend the money which the people of this country think is given to her. I am not now finding

* To which must now be added £10,000, on his marriage.

fault with a cook at £700 a-year, and a poet at £100. But I do object to a lot of political sinecurists, changing with the Ministry, who draw away a large portion of the sum voted to her. There is a Lord Steward who gets £2,000 a-year for doing nothing, and there is a Treasurer who gets £904 per annum to help him. A Comptroller with the same salary is equally a sinecurist. The Lord Chamberlain, at £2,000 a-year, and the Vice-Chamberlain, at £924, may both be dispensed with to the advantage of everybody; while, I am sure, the eight sergeants-at-arms, whose duties are "to hold watch outside the royal tent, in complete armour, with bow, arrows, sword, and mace of office, and to capture any traitor about the Court," ought now to be relegated to the British Museum; and as the Queen does not indulge in the pastime of hawking, I do not see why she is called upon to pay £1,200 a-year to an Hereditary Grand Falconer; to say nothing of the Master of the Buckhounds (a political sinecure), £1,700 a-year; the Master of the Horse, £2,500 a-year; Pages of the Back Stairs, Ladies of the Bed-chamber, Women of the Bedchamber, Gentlemen of the Wine and Beer Cellar, Clerk of the Kitchen, Maids of Honour, and a host of others. I suppose all those officers are supposed to add to the honour and dignity of the Crown. At any rate, the appointments are generally given to persons selected from that class which is continually prating about the honour and dignity of the throne. I think it would be more becoming on their part,—would better show their attachment to the throne and loyalty to the monarch,—if they were content with the honour and privilege of living within the splendid glitter of a Court for nothing, instead of receiving large salaries for now and again having the privilege of loitering within the precincts of Royalty. Their rapacity knows no bounds. E. G., writing to the *Daily News*, says : " When the Sultan visited this country he incurred a serious expense by giving snuff-boxes, covered with diamonds, to the officials of the Court. One noble lord, who had a situation about the Palace, bitterly complained that he had been left out of the distribution, and actually, like a sturdy beggar, whined and begged to the Grand Vizier until he got his snuff-box. Many suggestions have been made respecting the best method of receiving the Shah of Persia, so as to give him a befitting idea of our national characteristics. I would suggest that all persons who receive salary from the State be absolutely forbidden to levy black mail on him. This, after the experience, through which he is passing, of the rapacity of Continental countries, will agreeably surprise him, and prove to him that there is some difference between us and our neighbours. When an Oriental Potentate makes a present to one of our East Indian officials, the present is handed over to the public treasury, and he receives in return a gift exactly equal in value. Our diplomatists are allowed to receive neither decorations nor presents. Why should not this rule be extended to courtiers? Some strong measure ought to be taken to prevent the unblushing greed of these gentry producing upon our Persian guests the same feeling of disgust that was produced by a similar exhibition of rapacity on the minds of the Ministers of the Sultan. The 'no fees to servants,' which is inscribed on the walls of some places of public amusement, ought to be prominently inscribed over Buckingham Palace and Windsor Castle. I trust that before the arrival of the Shah some member of the House of Commons will obtain a distinct assurance that neither directly nor indirectly will he have to pay for his lodgings in Buckingham Palace. Courtiers receive handsome salaries for doing very little. It is insufferable that our hospitality should be marred by their pretensions to be paid for it." If appointments without work were also without pay, I believe there would be crowds of lords

THE NATIONAL EXPENDITURE. 175

and ladies only too happy to do for nothing that which is now so well paid for. Perhaps then there might be something saved out of the Royal Household expenses towards providing a dowry whenever a royal marriage takes place, without the painful operation of screwing it out of John Bull, who, it seems, is not now inclined to pay without a grumble. Of course, I am aware that the present system is fixed by Act of Parliament; but I have yet to learn that our laws are so perfect that they cannot be altered, or that an Act passed in the dark ages cannot be repealed now.

I think, gentlemen, that I have now shown you that our expenditure is recklessly extravagant, and so long as the present system exists must be so. If I were asked how I would reduce the vast expenditure of this country, my answer would be that I would consult the permanent Heads of the Departments. I would go, for instance, to the Duke of Cambridge, and I would say to him, "Your Royal Highness receives £16 a day as a Field Marshal; as General Commanding-in-Chief, £7 per diem; as three Colonels rolled into one, viz., as Colonel of the Artillery, as Colonel of the Engineers, and as Colonel of the Grenadier Guards, at least £2,000 a year; and your Royal Highness must not forget the pension of

£12,000 a year which you receive; making a total of £22,395 per annum, which is more, your Royal Highness, than the gentry and trading community of the city of Norwich pay in Income Tax;" and then I would add, "So that I think your Royal Highness knows, if you be honest, where to recommend a reduction in the army estimates." Could not the Horse Guards and the War Office between them, think you, find out where the estimates might be reduced two and-a-half millions? Could not the Admiralty, if they wished, find out where a similar sum might be saved? Then, if the Pension List be reduced by two millions, and a saving effected in Law Courts of one million by the introduction of the system of the fees covering the expenses, and two millions knocked off the Civil Service expenditure, there would be a saving of ten millions. How much do the English people cost governing? Why, one-fifth of the amount expended. I would have you remember that more than two-fifths of the expenditure are on behalf of the National Debt; other two-fifths are for National Defences, and only one-fifth is required for the actual government of the country. If the Heads of the Departments think that the reductions I have mentioned cannot safely be effected, let a Finance Committee of the House of

Commons try its hand. Every other public body in the kingdom, town council, parish vestry, railway board, and even chapels have found it indispensable to have a Finance Committee. Only the House of Commons, in its wisdom, which passeth all understanding, sees that it matters little how much business it undertakes,—matters still less what affairs it meddles with,—and matters nothing at all how many millions it spends.

Inasmuch as the public expenditure and taxation are national and not party questions, members of both sides of the House ought to sit on that committee. It should be formed of the most capable men of business. The committee should be appointed permanently for the duration of the House appointing it; and it should sit more or less day by day during the session, and should have the power to sit during the recess. A committee like this, with its powers well defined, would not only have a great tendency to economise the expenditure, but it would relieve the House of Commons from a deal of work which now impedes necessary reforms.

But, after all, gentlemen, it is a question for the constituencies, and that is why Direct Taxation would be such a good thing. It would make the constituencies feel they were taxpayers. The representatives would then soon become economisers. The influence of a constituency over its members is very great. Even a good liberal like Mr. Walter Morrison is not beyond this influence. I remember hearing him say, at Plymouth, in 1872, that his constituency preferred an extravagant Government. Of course, Plymouth is a peculiar town, being a garrison town and close to a dockyard, so that what is sport for Plymouth is death for the taxpayer. "During the eleven years," said Mr. Morrison, "that I have had the honour of representing Plymouth, I have only received a single letter pointing out a mode of reducing the expenditure of the State, and that letter was from Sir William Hamilton; but within the same period hundreds of letters have come to me pressing for a larger expenditure on the part of the Government." When influence like this is brought to bear on so sound a politician as Mr. Morrison, I think it is high time to enlighten those people who have eyes and yet do not see, but who vote at parliamentary elections.

Gentlemen, I have spoken of a reduction in the expenditure of £10,000,000. I have fixed upon that sum because those well able to judge — John Bright on the one hand, Lord Derby on the other — have stated that the expenditure ought to be reduced by that amount.

Have you ever asked yourselves what an enormous sum ten millions is? Have you ever calculated the good it might do? It would pay £1 a week for twelve months to every able-bodied pauper in England and Wales, and to 50,000 men besides. Can anyone doubt that if the £10,000,000 now withdrawn from production, and wasted, were productively employed, they would enable a great number of persons to work who are now idle, and increase to an enormous amount the material prosperity of the empire. Sir Charles Dilke has well said, "Rather than help the next generation to fight, I would prefer to so leave taxation as to make it hard for them to do so." Give a Government only as much as is necessary for carrying on the affairs of the nation, leaving the rest—the ten millions we are speaking of—to be employed productively, and such a stimulus will be given to trade, so many more men will be employed, and the difficulty of finding soldiers will be so great, that a great incentive to fighting will be removed. It is a well established fact, that in prosperous times, recruits are difficult to find. Men, instead of enlisting, obtain employment and improve their condition. They seek comforts for the inward and the outward man. They improve their homes. It has been observed, "As the homes, so the people." There is no crime in happy homes, and that statesman who will lift out from the depths of vice, and misery, and idleness, those who now are a standing reproach to the civilised age in which we live, will receive thanks expressed with such a sincere sense of gratitude from the country he has benefited, compared to which the praises sung in honour of the noblest achievements of the philanthropists, though uttered with the tongues of men and of angels, will be but as sounding brass and as tinkling cymbals.

VI.

A Plan of Direct Taxation.

No sooner had the Financial Reform Association issued its programme in 1848 than the question was raised on all hands, "What does the Association propose to substitute?" and from that day to this the question has been repeated over and over again. The Financial Reform Association has always, and, I think, very wisely, declined to answer that question. It started with a destructive policy, and it left, and still leaves, to others the task of pursuing a constructive policy. "It is not easy to see," says Mr. J. Alun Jones, "why the Association should be called upon to do what, so far as I know, has not been required from others. I have never heard that the Anti-Corn Law League were at any time called upon to propose duties in lieu of the Corn Tax they sought to abolish, or that the advocates of the Permissive Bill are now asked to suggest any taxes to fill up the alarming deficit that would be caused by a suppression of the sale of intoxicating drinks. For myself, I think it will be soon enough to propound a scheme when the principles of the Association are adopted, and that the council, like doctors, need not prescribe until they are called in." When an unjust, an anomalous, and a clumsy system of raising the revenue exists, there is a definite task in accomplishing its downfall and pointing out the principle of the remedy, without going into details. A great many persons may agree that a system is wrong, and may all unite for its overthrow, but they may all differ as to what is to take its place, and when the task of reconstruction begins they may range themselves on different sides. In the following remarks, therefore, it must be understood that I am speaking independently, and I do not commit the Association I represent. Nor, indeed, do I pin my faith to any scheme yet proposed. It is the duty of the Government to discover a plan. The Chancellor of the Exchequer is paid £5,000 a year to find out how to raise the money. All I have endeavoured to do has been to point out the gross injustice and the great improvidence of the existing scheme, and for the plan which I shall place before you I claim no merit. I am not the author of it. Indeed, it is not a new one, but it seems to me to be the best which has yet been suggested, and I therefore submit it to your consideration. I will willingly desert it for a better. However it may fall short of perfection, I am sure of one thing, that no system can be perfect which is not purely and entirely a direct system. I cannot accept the dogma — for it is nothing but a dogma — that a thing may be right in theory, but wrong in practice. If a thing be theoretically right, it cannot be practically wrong. First satisfy yourself that your theory is right, and then diligently, though perhaps slowly, and minutely, yet comprehensively, work out your theory to its utmost limit, and its practicability will soon display itself. If a man were going to propose a new scheme, and had the two plans before him, would he, think you, select the indirect method? We collect our local rates on the direct system, and it works well. "Is there," asks Mr. C. E. Macqueen, "one sane man within the four seas of Britain who, knowing the operation and effects of the two systems of Taxation, would wish to see our Direct mode of providing for local exigencies exchanged for the Indirect one? We greatly doubt it." Parishes, local board districts, boroughs, and counties raise all the rates by direct imposts. There may be complaints of the amount of the rates, and of the assessment of the houses, but there is no grumbling at the way it is collected ; and the British ratepayer would stand aghast if it were proposed to tax his food and his comforts by a sort of *octroi* dues, in order that the streets might be lighted, the roads paved, and the poor fed.

I am not exaggerating when I say that there have been scores of plans proposed as substitutes for the present method of raising the revenue. So far as most of them are concerned, however, the mere mention of them is sufficient to ensure their condemnation, and it serves to show how miserably defective the existing system must be when the merest crotchets can find supporters, not because the plans have any intrinsic merit, but because it is believed that any method whatever must be better than the one we have at present, than which nothing can be worse. An export duty on coal is seriously proposed and advocated, as if the country was so steeped in stupidity that it would return to the flint rifle and wooden ships—for there is just as much sense in the one proposal as the other. Some propose a license on every trade, according to its status, which would be "harassing every trade and worrying every profession" with a vengeance, while others, with equal acumen, gravely suggest a poll tax, to be levied, heaven knows how, and collected by the Lord Nozoo.

We have a tax on income, and there can be no doubt that an Income Tax would be the fairest, the most just, and the most equitable way of raising the entire revenue—if all men were honest, and were known to be honest. But men, unfortunately, are rather otherwise than honest, and in that state of affairs a just Income Tax, or a tax on capitalised incomes or on capitalised property (both of which are proposed) is impossible, in spite of Mr. Muntz's suggestion, that the State should have the right of pre-emption. A tax on expenditure is open to the same objections; while a tax upon wages is simply impossible. Mr. Samuel Hand, of Wolverhampton, suggests, as a substitute for the Income Tax, that the present receipt stamp of one penny value should be imperative in all transactions involving the payment of from two pounds to ten pounds; and that every additional ten pounds or fraction of ten pounds should require a further penny stamp. This system would, he asserts, realise a larger sum than the present Income Tax, at the same time that it would be less felt, would be unerring in its application, and would dispense with returns of incomes having to be made. Mr. Hand is evidently one of those who believe that a tax, however levied, ultimately falls on profits, and he thinks, therefore, that the best plan is to tax profits at once. The proposal, however, is open to the objections which are urged against all stamps; and, however useful as a substitute "until something better turns up," will never be made the means of raising by far the largest amount of our revenue, which is what we want at present. Some gentlemen imagine that, as the National Debt was incurred by the propertied classes and for the propertied classes, therefore property should at any rate pay the whole of the interest of that debt; while there are others who think that property ought to bear the entire revenue of the country.

The last-mentioned scheme is propounded by the very highest authorities,—Locke, Turgot, and Dr. Chalmers. "If," says Chalmers, " the whole of our public revenue were raised by means of a territorial impost, it would ultimately add nothing to the burden which now lies on the proprietors of the land, for they, when fighting against such a commutation, are fighting in defence of an imaginary interest." The upholders of this principle, as far as I can make them out, belong to two classes; those who, like Locke, maintain that all taxes, however levied, fall on the land at last, and may therefore just as well be laid there at first; and another class, whose name is Legion, who believe that a tax on land has the very interesting, peculiar, and desirable quality of not falling upon anybody's shoulders at all. Another proposal is, that all property whatsoever, castles, mills, houses, chairs, tables and saucepans should be valued and taxed. The aggregate value of all these things, it is said, is £14,000,000,000, of which £10,000,000,000 could be rated at, say, 1½d., which at once produces a revenue of £63,000,000, which, with what is got from the Post Office, is all that is required.

There seems to be a lingering desire in this country to tax dull, inanimate property. The existence of the Probate Duties shows it. But if property, rather than the man who owns it, is to bear the tax, by all means tax it when it is realised, not while it is being acquired. "As every tax must necessarily abstract a positive quantity of existent capital from private use for public benefit, the taking of that quantity from the *growth* leaves the power of reproduction untouched and unimpaired. The fruit, not the tree; the milk, not the cow; the fare, not the cab; the hire, not the horse, is what ought to be subject to taxation." Let us tax wealth when it is made, not the process of making wealth. It may be objected that such an impost would be a tax on providence, and would induce people not to save.

That, however, seems to me very much like saying that a man would object to receive payment of money due to him because he would have to buy a receipt stamp. At present land pays almost nothing to the imperial revenue, beyond what its owners pay as Income Tax; and although land constantly increases in value, without any exertion on the part of the owners, while they sleep, as Mr. Mill puts it, yet that increase gives no corresponding contributions towards the public expenditure. There can be no doubt it would be a very good thing to tax the land, if only to make the owners cultivate it, and so provide more, and consequently cheaper, food for the people of this country. Of the seventy-four million acres which the British Islands contain, only about forty-two millions are laid out as arable land or good pasture; while about thirty millions of these acres are almost unenclosed, and scarcely redeemed from their natural condition. Of this vast surface some portions, of course, are barren mountain or deep bog; but the aggregate of these descriptions would certainly not amount to five millions of acres. There remain, at all events, twenty-five millions of acres which present no insuperable physical difficulties to the work of cultivation; and which, if they could be cultivated successfully, would increase by more than half, the present power of this kingdom to support its teeming population. Add to this the fact, as the Earl of Derby stated, that the land might produce twice as much as it does — and it would, I maintain, if it were taxed — and we find that three times as much food ought to be produced in this country as is produced at present.

I do not, however, think it wise to consider property, which, under our political system is after all a commodity, as a something to be taxed. It may be taken as a standard or a criterion of a man's ability to pay a certain amount, but it is unwise to speak of taxing it. The proper thing to tax is neither land, nor wages, nor profits, but the Man, the Citizen. Yet the principle of taxing property is acknowledged — in the Probate Duties, for instance. Why should an additional tax be imposed because the owner of a property is dead. The man when living paid his taxes, and the successor to his estates will also pay, and why the State should step in and take out a sort of "soke" simply because the estate is changing hands, is neither reasonable nor equitable. There is another injustice also in connection with this, which, although not bearing directly on my present argument, is yet a branch of "Financial Reform" that ought not to be forgotten. As you are probably aware, there is great inequality in the method by which Probate and Succession Duties are levied. In the first place, not only does real estate escape, as a rule, while personal property is heavily mulcted, but large estates are assessed for Probate Duty at a less rate than small ones. Thus £1,000 has to pay at the rate of three per cent.; £10,000 at the rate of two per cent.; and £50,000 at the rate of one and a half per cent. The heaviest burdens are thus imposed upon those who have the least means. The extension of the Probate Duty, too, to real property would, if the duties are to exist at all, bring in a very large sum of money to the exchequer, compared to what is now the case. Let me give a few instances. Supposing a real estate of £70,000 passes to a nephew, aged twenty-five years, he would have to pay £810; but if a personal estate of £70,000 passes to a brother and sister, aged respectively sixty-five and seventy-five, they would have to pay no less than £3,890, while if the nephew in the former case had been of the same age as either of the others, he would only have had to pay £300. The tax is even more oppressive to the poorer classes. If a poor man leaves £200 to his family, they have to pay Probate Duty £8, Succession Duty £2, and legal expenses £4 12s., making a total of £14 12s., which is at the rate of £7 6s. per cent.. Is not this, therefore, a tax pressing with undue severity upon the widow and the fatherless? In 1871 two wills were proved, each of them relating to property worth more than a million, viz., those of Mr. Thornton, in England, and Mr. Baird, in Scotland. Had the property been personal property, the probate duty on each would have been £15,000 or thereabouts; but, being real property, not a penny found its way into the national exchequer. In 1859, Mr. Bright put this injustice very plainly before the House of Commons. He said, "I was fortunate enough to have a small property left to me by a person of whom I had no knowledge. I never saw him. He was an old gentleman, a great friend of peace, and opposed to the Russian war; and seeing that my honourable friend, the member for Rochdale, and myself were very strenuous in our opposition to that war, he did what was in his power to mark his opinion of the course we had taken. I sold the property for £1,400 or £1,500; and when I came to pay my Legacy Duty—that is, the Succession Tax—I was greatly astonished at the small sum I had to pay. My age was taken, an estimate of the annual value of the property was made, and I was told that I had to pay something like £40 or £50. If the property had been in the Funds, or invested in any other of the modes to which I have referred, I should have had to pay £140 at least. Take the case of an honourable gentleman on this side the House, who has been more fortunate than myself. A property worth £32,000 was left to him by a person who was not a blood relation. If it had been in the Funds, or in ships, or in railways, or employed in trade, the Succession Duty would have amounted to £3,200. What did he pay? He is not an old man — probably younger than the average of members in this House—and yet, upon the property being valued, and a calculation made of the number of years he might live, he found that he had to pay, not £3,200, but £700."

Pardon this digression. I will now proceed with the argument. Having laid down the rule that the citizen and nothing else should be taxed, let us see by what criteria we can ascertain how much he ought to pay. What are the rules which should regulate taxation?

 1st. There should be "equality of taxation." Every man should pay his share in proportion to the protection he receives, that is, according to his means. This is sometimes called making an "equal sacrifice," which means that the rich man — however wealthy he may be — should be taxed to such an amount that he will feel the pressure just as much as the poor man feels the few shillings or pounds that are wrung from his meagre earnings.

2nd. The tax which each individual should be called upon to pay ought to be certain, and not arbitrary or voluntary.

3rd. The time when taxes are to be collected ought to be well known.

4th. Every tax ought to be so contrived as both to take out and keep out of the pockets of the people as little as possible over and above what it brings into the Treasury of the State.

5th. No tax should prevent the increase of the fund from which the taxes are paid, nor should it deny to any man his natural right to the free exchange of the fruits of his labour.

6th. The standard of valuation and assessment ought to be certain, visible, and tangible; not invisible, incorporeal, and intangible.

7th. Persons with barely sufficient means to provide the necessaries of life, and no more, should not be taxed at all.

I have on other occasions treated of the first five. I propose now to say a few words on the ~~fifth~~ *seventh* and sixth.

Now, what is there on the very outset which occurs to one as being certain, visible, and tangible in regard to a man's ability to pay a tax? Not his income, for that often fluctuates; it is therefore uncertain: there are no means of ascertaining it; it is therefore invisible. A man's property is the best criterion of his ability to pay a tax for the protection of that property. I do not mean his land only. I mean all realised property, such as railway shares, bank shares, canal shares, and all other shares, as well as, perhaps, ships. A tax on persons owning property in proportion to the property they possess could not be oppressive if £30,000,000 were raised from them. I hope I shall hear nothing about the increased burdens on land. If the landowners of this country wish the question to be enquired into, they will find it bad for the view they take of the question. I am anxious to avoid any discussion that might seem tinctured with too strong an opinion of the past conduct of the aristocracy. The landowners of to-day are not responsible for the wickedness and the crimes of their ancestors, any more than the other classes of society can be blamed for the follies of their progenitors. It is only, therefore, when I hear the "rights of property" talked of by those who have no "rights" at all, except possession gained by might, that I am induced to remind them of Cobden's words, "I warn the aristocracy not to force the people to look into the subject of Taxation—not to force them to see how they have been robbed, plundered, and bamboozled for ages by them." Why should the landholders oppose such a scheme? I have pointed out the immense material advantages which would follow the adoption of Free Trade. Land would be the first thing to rise in value. If its value were only increased by one-fifth, how much would the landholder with £20,000 a year lose by a tax of 4s. in the pound? Say rather, How much would he gain? Let him work out this simple sum, and he will become a Free Trader. The tax, however, would not be anything like so much as that, because I am not proposing that landowners should be the only persons taxed, but that the owners of other sorts of realised property whatsoever should bear their share.

There is, then, a simple way of reaching all those persons who have property. But there are several persons who have no property. By far the greater number of these, however, are householders; and here again we have something "certain, tangible, and visible" upon which to base a tax. The value of a house is always known, and the rent is, as a rule, a fair criterion of the amount of taxation a man is able to bear. Some people may think that an Inhabited House Duty, as it is improperly called, would be a tax upon rent, and would fall upon the owner. I cannot admit that. Why is not the same assertion made with regard to local rates? If the owners of empty houses had to pay, it might then be said the tax fell upon rental; or if a house duty in addition to the present taxes were imposed, perhaps rents might be affected. But I am not proposing an additional tax. I am proposing a small and cheaply collected tax, as a substitute for a large and expensively collected one. The taxpayer would derive a benefit by the change, and if he made any move at all, it would be to a better and a larger house, and thus rents would be beneficially affected. Nothing can be more certain than that the tenant pays the rent. It is equally certain he would pay the tax. For my own part, I cannot see that if a man pays a tax of £2 because he lives in a house of £30 a year rent, that is a tax upon his house, or is paid by his landlord, any more than if, living in that house, he pays an Income Tax of £2 because his income is £250 a year. A tax on persons living in houses is merely saying to a man, "You live in a house of such a rent, therefore you can afford to pay so much tax." The incidence of the tax is upon the tenant alone, and can no more be said to be a tax upon the owner, or upon the rent, than the rise in the price of coal and meat, or the increase of a man's family with no increase of income, thus obliging him to remove to a cheaper house, causing rents to fall, can be said to be a tax upon the owner.

There are in England and Wales and Scotland 4,976,074 inhabited houses; to these have to be added those in Ireland and the smaller islands; and I think there can be no doubt that, without any oppression, £28,000,000 might be raised from their occupants, which, added to the £30,000,000 from the land, and to the amount obtained from the Post Office, Telegraphs, Crown Lands, etc., makes the total of what ought to be raised for the government of the country. Let us put down the inhabited houses in Great Britain and Ireland at 6,000,000 (which is under the mark); then, roughly speaking, the annual tax upon persons living in

200,000 houses under £5 rent would be 10s. each =	£100,000
300,000 „ „ 10 „ „ 20s. „ =	300,000
400,000 „ „ 20 „ „ 40s. „ =	800,000

A PLAN OF DIRECT TAXATION.

500,000 houses under £40 rent	would be	60s. each	=	1,500,000
1,000,000 „	„	60 „	„	80s. „	=	4,000,000
1,300,000 „	„	80 „	„	100s. „	=	6,500,000
1,200,000 „	„	100 „	„	120s. „	=	6,000,000
700,000 „	„	200 „	„	160s. „	=	5,600,000
300,000 „	„	300 „	„	180s. „	=	2,700,000
100,000 houses above 300	„	„	200s. „	=	1,000,000

£28,500,000

Now, I ask any man living in a £20 house whether he would not prefer to pay £2 per annum direct, rather than the much larger sum that is now obtained from him by the present indirect method? I ask the tenants of other houses a similar question? It is sometimes said that it would be impossible to collect such a tax from the homes of the very poor. The rents, however, are collected, and I venture to think that Government would be able to collect the Queen's taxes just as well as the rent collector gets his master's rents. The tenants, it is true, might not like the process at first, but "use doth breed a habit in a man," and the people would soon find out that what cannot be cured must be endured, and that they would be paying less by this method than they had previously paid.

Again, there are four and a half millions of inhabited houses in England and Wales. The number of married men in England and Wales was, at the time of the Census, 3,883,363; so that a tax on those who live in houses would include a large number of bachelors; and a great many of the poorer class would be reached by a tax on those who live in flats or tenements, which would be regulated by their rent, just as if they lived in houses. There is, of course, a balance left of those who seemingly escape taxation. Some of them, however, are property owners, and pay that way; others are very poor, and are entitled to escape under the fifth of the rules I laid down; while the rest, who of course must be lodgers, would pay indirectly through their "landlord," as he is called, in the rent they pay him. I acknowledge that so far as these are concerned, this is the weak point of the system I advocate, because an indirect tax of such a nature has at least one-half of the disadvantages of a tax on commodities. I have little doubt that the wisdom of the Legislature can find out some direct method of reaching them. Whether or not, I would much rather that a few should escape, in order that the great mass may be fairly taxed, rather than that a great number of the poor should be heavily oppressed, in order that all may be reached. I do not know what may be the opinion of legislators and statesmen, but the opinion I hold is this, that it would be much better to have a less taxed and more comfortable *residuum* of people, even if their wealthier brethren had to pay a little more than their share, than a class of poor, as at present, more highly taxed in proportion to their means than the richest noble in the land, and the landowners of the country paying as little as they possibly can. I am not sure, either, that more would escape under the proposed plan than at present. The number of males in England and Wales above 25 years of age (less paupers, prisoners, soldiers, and others who don't pay taxes) was at the last Census 4,578,882. The number of inhabited houses in the same year was 4,259,117. I should like to know how many teetotallers the Temperance societies claim for that year. I am sure there are more than 319,765 teetotallers, males of full age, in England, and yet not all that number would escape a tax on householders. I venture to think that those figures show that more persons escape their share of taxation by abstaining from intoxicating drinks, under the present system, than would escape under the system of which I am speaking.

Another advantage in the system I am advocating would be the cheapness of collecting. There would be no other expense but that of actual collection. The Hon. D. Wells, the great American financier, has pointed out, too, that in the case of persons who are both owners and occupiers, one assessment would do for both taxes. Thus—

Value of place of business	£10,000
Three times rent of building (£1,000) as basis of tax as occupier . .	3,000
Total valuation for assessment . .	£13,000

It may be said that this proposal is one for too great a change to be accomplished at once. To that objection I reply that my friend, Mr. J. Alun Jones, of Liverpool, who has paid great attention to the whole subject, has prepared a "draft budget," which, to my mind, might be accomplished to-morrow. Mr. Jones does not, of course, intend his scheme to be a final one, and he is quite open to consider any amendments. His budget, however, if I may be allowed to call it one, includes an entire substitution of direct for indirect taxation. He proposes to abolish all duties of Customs and Excise and Stamps, to sweep away the Custom-houses, thus saving a great deal of the cost of collection, and allowing the free development of the trade of the country by unrestricted commerce, thus carrying out the principle contained in the Magna Charta.* Camilla, we are told, could glide over a field of corn without bending a stem; thus lightly, says M. Dureau, should taxation fall on all that pertains to industry. Mr. Jones' "budget" would do this, and I recommend it as a great stride in the direction of the policy I am advocating.†

Although, then, this scheme which I advocate is very imperfect, it is infinitely nearer perfection than the present system. True, it would allow some to escape taxation who could well afford to pay their fair share, but is not that better than highly to tax everybody in order that the poorest may be reached? Whatever may be the disadvantages of the proposal, it is fraught with such advantages as ought to commend it to all who have the welfare of their country at heart. Such a system would prevent no man from getting an honest living, as indirect taxes always must; it would allow the production and the distribution of wealth to proceed according to natural laws, untrammelled on the one hand, stimulated on the other;

* All merchants shall have safe and secure conduct to go out of, and to come into England, and to stay there, and to pass as well by land as by water, for buying and selling by the ancient and allowed customs, without any evil tolls. *Magna Charta.*

† See Appendix B.

industry would be free; taxes would be cheaply collected, and the material prosperity of this country would be so immensely increased, that homes would be happier, people more contented, and vice and misery diminished in such an enormous degree, that philanthropists and statesmen would think they had found a panacea for all the squalor and wretchedness which are now seen in such close proximity to wealth and luxury.

APPENDIX A.

WHILE these pages were in the press, Sir Stafford Northcote introduced his Budget, abolishing the sugar duties. Many of the arguments used in the text were used during the debates on that policy as well as in the public prints. On the morning of the very day the Budget was introduced into the Committee (April 16th, 1873), the *Daily News* laid great stress upon the annoyance to various trades, as pointed out in the text at page 36, by stating that, "Ever since the advent of the new Government became certain, particular trades have been kept almost in a state of stagnation, waiting to learn what changes would be made in the Customs. The sugar trade, in which large stocks are necessarily held by merchants and refiners, has been almost paralysed." What is alone surprising is that obtuseness which acknowledges that the abolition of the sugar duties is good for the country, and yet fails to see that a similar policy in regard to tea or any other taxed commodity would be equally beneficial. Mr. Gladstone described the increased prosperity which has always followed the remission of a duty, as "something approaching to magic;" and he also spoke favourably of there now being a chance of the cultivation of sugar in this country from beet "and other commodities." The Chancellor of the Exchequer, too, said that it was to be hoped that the abolition of the sugar duties would not only be followed by an increase in the consumption of sugar, but that there would be " elasticity in tea, coffee, and other articles of consumption." All this supports the views propounded in this book, while the

following anecdote from Sir Stafford Northcote's speech shows how easily the frauds by Custom-house officers, as mentioned on page 38. can be carried on. The right hon. gentleman said—
"I will mention a story which I heard a few days ago. I was told by a friend of mine that he met a gentleman who said to him, 'I have a cargo of sugar at this moment coming to this country. It depends upon the decision of an officer of the Customs, who knows nothing about it, whether it should be put in one class or another, and according as it is put in one class or another I will either make or lose by the cargo, £1,200.'"
I will merely add that I have been informed that the abolition of the sugar duties will enable the staff at the Liverpool Custom-house alone to be reduced by sixty clerks, to say nothing of other officials, and the clerks which every merchant in the trade has to keep on purpose to transact Custom-house business.

I would like to refer to Mr. Rathbone's speech on Mr. Cross's Licensing Bill, as strengthening the arguments on the liquor question used in the first chapter of this book. The Hon. Member points out that when there was virtually Free Trade in liquor in the town he represents (1862 to 1866), drunkenness greatly decreased; and that when the policy was departed from the number of convictions for that offence at once increased ten per cent.

APPENDIX B.

By J. ALUN JONES, Esq.,
BARRISTER-AT-LAW, LIVERPOOL.

I HERE submit what I may call a draft budget, embodying the principles of Free Trade, and showing how they would, if applied, have affected the finances of a given year. I have selected 1867, not because there are any special features in the accounts of that year that make them exceptionally easy to deal with, but because Mr. Dudley Baxter's work on the income of the nation gives the figures for that year, and also because there is no subsequent year of the financial history of which so much can be ascertained on Government authority.

A few words of explanation may be needful as to the mode in which this sketch has been drawn up. The first column, headed "Actual," contains the figures of the finance accounts for 1867, as prepared by Mr. Henry Lloyd Morgan, and published in the *Financial Reform Almanack*. The second column, headed "Proposed," shows how the various items would have been altered or have disappeared, and a substitute provided in a direct taxation budget.

The first to be noticed is the income side of the sheet. In this the sources of revenue, headed respectively Customs, Excise, Stamps and Assessed Taxes, disappear, while the Post Office, Crown Lands, and Miscellaneous are, of course, retained. The Land Tax is merged in the first class of taxes on income from capital (Schedule A.) The amount of the tax, four shillings in the pound, is simply that fixed by the Acts of 1692, and so shamelessly nullified a few years afterwards by the Landlords' Parliament of that time. The basis of the calculation is taken from Mr. Dudley Baxter's work, which puts the income of the nation from those sources that come under Schedule A (land, houses, mines, etc.,) at £162,500,000. This, at four shillings in the pound, gives £32,500,000, as stated.

The next class, Schedule C (incomes from the public funds), is fixed by the same authority at thirty-four millions. This tax is objected to by many, on the ground that it is unfair to tax the public creditor, but as the regularity and certainty of payment of interest on a national debt depend on the stability and good administration of Government, it certainly seems to me quite just to require some small contribution from fundholders towards securing such advantages. The same reasons apply with even greater force to the holders of offices and pensions, who come under Schedule E, for they, without any investment of capital at all, receive a sure and regular income from the nation, and, so far as the advantages enjoyed are concerned, they are in almost as good a position as persons deriving an income from land, the main difference in effect on themselves being that they do not, like landowners, share the benefit of increasing incomes as a result of growing national wealth and prosperity. I should add that the figures on which the calculation for Schedule E is based have been taken from the *Statistical Abstract*, No. xviii., page 16.

I now come to the last class of taxes, taxes on occupation. I may be permitted to cite the opinion of Mr. Wells, the eminent American financier, who states in his *Report on Taxation in the State of New York*, that rental is by far the surest indication of the wealth of individuals, and of their relative ability to pay taxes. There is much difficulty in getting at reliable figures whereon to base an estimate for this tax. I have calculated £145,536,081 to be the gross rental of the United Kingdom, by taking first the gross estimated rental of England (*Financial Reform Almanack*, 1870, p. 43), in 1867, £118,384,081, and then the national income of Scotland and Ireland as compared with that of England, as the basis of a simple proportion sum by which to find the proportionate rental of those countries. The results, added to the rental of England, give the above figures. The rate, if an honest assessment were made, might be much less, for as is well known, a large number of country houses, especially those of our county magnates, are rated at sums absurdly small compared with their real value.

In dealing with the expenditure, every item not connected with disbursements on account of indirect taxation is retained, the subject of economical administration being one into which I cannot now enter. The cost of the Army and Navy in the "Proposed" column is lessened by £739,000, the expense of the Coastguard fleet and service, which are included in the Navy estimates for the obvious purpose of hoodwinking the public as to the real cost of the Custom-house system. The cost of collecting and managing the Customs disappears, and that of the Inland Revenue is reduced by a million, £310,000 being amply sufficient for the collection of direct taxes, which might very easily be entrusted to the collectors of local rates. A sum not ascertainable *should* be deducted from the amount paid for superannuation, some of which certainly goes to retired revenue officials. In the same way, deductions should be made from the cost of Public works and buildings, which includes Customhouses that would no longer be needful; and from the charge for law and justice on account of prosecuting and punishing offenders against the revenue laws. There are, also, other savings that could be pointed out as certain to accrue from the abolition of our Customs and Excise system; for instance, a loss of £352,000, which arises from the collection of revenue in 71 of our ports, would be avoided. The restoration of many thousand men employed by the Customs and Revenue departments to productive industry should also be taken into account.

One word as to the general results of this sketched budget. It means that, with such a mode of taxation as that asked for by the Financial Reform Association, the country would in 1867 have obtained for £72,381,560 what, under the present system, cost no less than £74,908,606, being a saving of two millions and a half. Add to this the enormous advantages of a complete liberation of trade from every trammel, and the fair distribution of the burden over all, not taxing the poor man according to his wants, while letting the rich off with an infinitely lighter load, but calling on all according to their ability and to the benefits they derive from well-ordered government to pay for it; and above all, the priceless moral benefit of spreading among the masses a conviction that the Government is dealing justly by them, a conviction which would be a stronger safeguard against revolution than any other policy that can be conceived.

FINANCE ACCOUNTS, ENDING MARCH 31st, 1868, AS THEY WERE AND AS THEY MIGHT HAVE BEEN.

INCOME.	ACTUAL.	PROPOSED.
Balances and Bills outstanding, and Advances repayable	3,180,497	3,180,497
1. Customs	22,664,980	Nil
2. Excise	20,190,338	Nil
3. Stamps	9,475,177	Nil
4. Land Tax	1,092,695	See below.
5. Assessed Taxes	2,360,301	Nil
6. Income Tax	6,184,166	See below.
7. Post Office	4,558,962	4,558,962
8. Crown Lands	449,252	449,252
9. Miscellaneous	2,586,218	2,586,218
Taxes on Income from Capital:—		
4s. in the £ on Schedule A. (Lands, &c.)		32,500,000
1s. in the £ on Schedule C (Annuities, &c.)		1,700,000
3s. in the £ on Schedule E. (Officers and Pensions)		3,593,012
Tax on Occupation 3s. 3d. in the £ on Rental		23,748,363
	72,742,586	72,316,304
Excess of Expenditure over Income	2,166,020	65,256

74,908,606   72,381,560

FINANCE ACCOUNTS, ENDING MARCH 31st, 1868, AS THEY WERE AND AS THEY MIGHT HAVE BEEN.

EXPENDITURE.	ACTUAL.	PROPOSED.
10. Interest and Management of National Debt	26,571,750	26,571,750
11. Army and Navy (cost of Customs, Fleet, and Service £739,000)	28,587,530	27,848,530
12. Cost of Collection and Management of Revenue Departments:—		
Customs	788,046	Nil.
Inland Revenue	1,310,026	310,026
Post Office	2,327,883	2,327,883
Superannuations	457,247	457,247
Packet Service	808,517	808,517
Crown Lands	95,780	95,780
13. Public Works and Buildings	722,393	722,393
14. Salaries and Expenses of Public Departments	1,846,670	1,846,670
15. Law and Justice	3,769,327	3,769,327
16. Education, Science, and Art	1,595,447	1,595,447
17. Colonial and Consular	718,777	718,777
18. Superannuations, &c.	372,946	372,946
19. Miscellaneous	216,982	216,982
20. Deficiency of Grants	79,829	79,829
21. Supplemental	159,000	159,000
22. Civil List	405,721	405,721
23. Annuities and Pensions	286,839	286,839
24. Interest on Loans, Secret Service, &c.	211,305	211,305
25. Fortifications	530,000	530,000
	71,862,015	69,334,969
Balances, &c., outstanding, and Repayable Votes	3,046,591	3,046,591
	74,908,606	72,381,560

INDEX.

Abolition of the Corn Laws, 6.
Admiralty, Jobbery at the, 135.
Alderney, Fortifications of, 141.
Appendix A, 204.
    Do. B, 206.
Army and Navy Expenditure, 126.
Autumn Manœuvres, 129.

Balance Sheet, National, 119.
Beer, Tax on, 3.
Beetroot, cultivation of, 32.
Blackstone on Excise Duties, 2.
Bookkeeping, National, 120, 166.
Bribery of Members of Parliament, 115.
Bright, J., on Drunkenness, 16.
    the National Stewards, 148.
    Expenditure, 113.
    Succession Duties, 191.
Budget, Draft of, 206.

Carey, H. C., on Protection, 97.
Cheap Wines a cause of temperance, 28.
Chicory, cultivation of, 34.
Circumlocution, 144.
Civil Service, discontent in, 167.
    examinations, 168.
    expenditure, 143.
Class Legislation, 3.

Coleridge, Lord, on Drunkenness, 16.
Committee of Supply, 114.
Cope, Bros., on Indirect Taxation, 8.
Corn Laws, Abolition of, 6.
Criteria of Taxation, 192.
Custom House, 82, 88.
    Officers, frauds by, 38, 205.
Customs abolished by Edward II., 2.
    curiosities of, 51.
    introduced by Edward I., 2.
    origin of, 2.
    prevent invention, 107.
    Strabo on, 2.

Derby, Earl of, on Reduction of Expenditure, 113.
Dilke, Sir C., on Incidence of Taxation, 61.
    Patronage, 117.
    War expenditure, 179.
Direct Taxation, 41, 177.
    advantages of, 41.
    check upon extravagance, 47.
    incidence of, 49.
    Macaulay, Lord, on, 41.
    no National Debt with, 43.
    plans of, 184.
    prevents war, 42.

Discontent in the Civil Service, 167.
Distress caused by Indirect Taxation, 5.
Dockyard Sales, 137.
Donnell, Robert, on Retaliatory Duties, 24.
Drunkard (the) Stumbling block to Free Trade, 15.
Drunkenness, J. Bright on, 16.
  cannot be prevented by Taxes, 15.
  Coleridge on, 16.
  in France, Jersey, &c., 27.
Duties prevent invention, 33.

Effects of Indirect Taxation, 1.
Effects of Remission of Duties, 6.
Elections, Governmental interference in, 169.
Emperor of China on taxing intoxicants, 25.
Examinations, Civil Service, 168.
Excise Duties, Blackstone on, 2.
  Johnson, Dr., on, 3.
  prevent invention, 107.
Expenditure, Army and Navy, 126.
  Civil Service, 143.
  National, 112.
  Reduction of, 178.
Expense of collecting Indirect Taxes, 9.
Extravagance, National, 149.

Fielden, Joshua, M.P., on Malt Tax, 29.
  patronage, 116.

Finance Committee, 176.
Financial Reform Association, policy of, 181.
"Five Alls," the, 170.
Fortifications of Alderney, 141.
Free Exchange, 108.
Free Trade, 74.
  advantages of, 100—109.
  in America, 96.
  in banking, 105.
  in the Colonies, 101.
  in land, 105.
  not yet accomplished, 75.
  Potter, E., on, 102.
  prevents War, 110, 111.
  Wells, Hon. D., on, 97.
French Treaty, 100.

Gladstone, W. E., on the Expenditure, 113.
  on Free Trade, 76.
Governmental Patronage, 115.

Hand, Mr. S., plan of Taxation, 185.
Honorary Colonels, 132.
Horses, loss on sale of, 133.
Householders, tax on, 195.

Incidence of Direct Taxes, 49.
  Taxation, 57.
Income Tax, 50, 185.
Increased consumption, benefits of, 78.
Indirect Taxation, 1.
  a surreptitious mode, 7, 12.
  Cope Bros. on, 8.
  distress caused by, 5.
  effects of, 1, 24.
  expense of collecting, 9.

Indirect Taxation falls on consumers, 9.
  injures the producer, 12.
  is voluntary, 13.
Influence of constituencies on their members, 178.
Intoxicants, taxes on, 14, 25.
Introductory, vii.
Invention prevented by duties, 33.

Jobbery at the Admiralty, 135.
  Vanity Fair on, 150.
Johnson, Dr., on Excise, 3.
Jones, J. Alun, Budget by, 206.

Law Courts, cost of, 159, 161.
Lawson, Sir W., on taxing intoxicants, 26.
Legacy duty, 190.
Leslie, T. E. Cliffe, on Indirect Taxation, 24.
Licenses, 35.
London, central position of, 109.
Luxuries, taxes on, 31, 107.

McCombie, M.P., on Patronage, 117.
Macqueen, C. E., 45.
  on Direct Taxation, 183.
  on War Expenditure, 46.
Malt Tax, 28.
Match Tax, 25.
Medway, sale of, 129.
Morrison, Walter, on Extravagence, 178.

National Balance Sheet, 119.
  Book-keeping, 120, 126.
National Debt, 122.

National Expenditure, 112.
  Stewards, 141.

Oath taken by pensioners, 168.
Officering of the Army, 132.
  Navy, 134.
Origin of Customs, 2.
Osborne, Bernal, on National Stewards, 141.

Patronage, 115.
  Secretary, 163.
Peace, 110.
Pelican, sale of, 129.
Pensions, 152.
Petition to H. of Commons, vii.
Plans of Direct Taxation, 184.
Post Office Scandal, 165.
Potter, E., on Free Trade, 102.
Premiums offered for subjects of taxation, 4.
Prince Christian's travelling expenses, 161.
Probate Duties, 189.
Property owners, tax on, 194.
Protection, H. C. Carey on, 97.
  Hon. D. Wells, on, 99.

Racking, 92.
Raper, J. H., on Voluntary Taxation, 13.
Recruiting, 170.
Reduction of Expenditure, 113, 175.
Remission of Duties, effects of, 6.
Reorganisation of Office, 143, 164.
Retaliatory duties, 24.
Retrograde policy proposed, 94.

Rewards by Government, 164.
Romilly Family, the, 152.
Royal Family, the, 171.
Rules of Taxation, 192.

Scudamore Scandal, 165.
Servants (Domestic) pay taxes, 70.
Sinecures, 149.
Smith, Sidney, on Taxation, 4.
Smuggling, 37, 39.
Spirits, Taxes on, 14.
Strabo on Customs, 2.
Succession Duties, 190.
Sugar duties, 32, 38, 204.

Tax on Beer, 3.
  on householders, 195.
  on imports, 103.
  on property owners, 194.
  on Spirits, 14, 25.
  on Sugar, 32, 204.

Tax on Tea, 32, 101.
  on Tobacco, 29.
Taxation, Criteria of, 192.
  of Working Class, 60.
  Middle Class, 67.
  Rules of, 192.
  Voluntary, 54.
Taxes, obligatory, 54.
  voluntary, 54.

Vanity Fair on Jobbery, 150.
Voluntary Taxation, 13
Voting Money on Account, 163.

War, 42, 46, 179.
Wells, Hon. D., on Free Trade, 97.
"Whip," 163.
Wine Trade, 84, 93, 107.
Worcester, not a port, 85.
Working Men and direct Taxation, 62, 66.

D. MARPLES, PRINTER, 50B, LORD STREET, LIVERPOOL.

www.ingramcontent.com/pod-product-compliance
Lightning Source LLC
Chambersburg PA
CBHW021844230426
43669CB00008B/1071